Praise for *Tested and Approved*

I've had the privilege of being led by Tom Lane since I was born, and for me (Blynda), since I married his son. There is no greater leader or pastor in our humble and unbiased opinion! As a father, his leadership has always been Spirit-led, consistent, and loving. Throughout my life, I've had men and women say to me, "I see your Dad like a father to me." And some of those people were older than him! *Tested and Approved* represents a father's perspective on ministry, and regardless of your age or experience, you will glean wisdom from a seasoned leader who is also an anointed father.

Todd and Blynda Lane
Son & Daughter-in-law
Executive Senior Pastor, Gateway Church

We have the privilege of calling Tom Lane our dad. He is one of the wisest and strongest leaders we know, and his input has laid the foundation for success in our lives and marriage. He lives the lessons he shares in this book, and his heart for people makes the insight he gives so valuable to anyone who receives it. He has guided many people during his 40 years in ministry with godly, biblical advice, enabling them to navigate life and ministry with great success. We have been greatly blessed by his wisdom, and we know that if you apply the lessons in this book, you too will be enriched by these lessons from our dad.

Braxton and Lisa Corley
Son-in-law & Daughter

In our experience, actual people rarely match up to the way they are perceived by others. However, Tom Lane defies what is typical. *Tested and Approved* beautifully describes the lessons he has taught and modeled for us to follow. This book is grounded in Scripture and perfectly describes the benefit of living a life submitted to our Lord. Each chapter provides memorable lessons we are attempting to model to this day, just as he has done for us.

Tyler and Marci Lane
Son & Daughter-in-law
Private Wealth Advisor, Merrill Private Wealth Management

I have always known my dad to be very intentional with his life. It's the attribute I admire most about him. Reading this book was another reminder of that intentionality. He refuses to sit back and just let life happen. Instead, he plans, he protects, and he preserves. He wrote this book to help others, but it's also a legacy to be passed down to each of us (his kids and grandkids). If you asked me to write out 21 lessons that I have learned from watching my dad live his life, they would have mirrored what is written in this book. Most importantly I am watching him "Finish Strong." He has not had a moment where he has "arrived." No, he has not stopped learning and growing, and I'm so grateful that I have been given a bird's-eye view into the amazing insight written in this book. Thank you, Dad!

Lindsay Lane Huckins
Daughter

Soon after Lindsay and I first starting dating, I told Tom that I was serious about his daughter. Tom and I began meeting almost on a weekly basis, and he would impart to me the lessons he had learned and was learning in his life. I remember soaking up the wisdom he was sharing because I was able to see the results of these lessons learned in and through his life. Now being married into the Lane family, I continue to learn and grow from watching how they encourage each other to pursue excellence in all areas, including personal and spiritual growth. I attribute so much of my leadership skills today to the one-on-one time I have had with Tom, learning the lessons outlined in this book. They truly have been tested and approved.

Brett Huckins
Son-in-law
Executive Director of Communications and Technology,
Gateway Church

I love this new book from my dear friend Tom Lane. We started in ministry together almost 40 years ago, and I can assure you this book is the fruit of Tom's personal life and how he lives. He practices what he teaches, and it is the reason he has been so successful on every level—personal, family, and ministry. I highly recommend this book and guarantee it will bless you and help you grow.

Jimmy Evans
Senior Pastor, Gateway Church
Best-selling Author and Speaker

Tom Lane is not only a colleague who has served with me in ministry for more than 20 years, but he's also one of my closest friends. He is one of the most teachable and humble men I know. I'm so glad Tom wrote this book because I know it will help many people learn how to navigate and avoid pitfalls and obstacles in life and in ministry. As you read this book, you'll find solid wisdom and biblical truth from a man who's spent the majority of his life walking in obedience to the Lord.

Robert Morris
Founding Lead Senior Pastor, Gateway Church
Best-selling Author of *The Blessed Life, Beyond Blessed,*
and *Take the Day Off*

Tom Lane is Tested and Approved. I've known him since 1981. While talking during one of our early lunches together, Tom was lining up his French fries from longest to shortest. I knew then this man had a divine purpose, which would include structure, process, consistency, and insight. Tom's sincere godliness has shaped his nuclear family, his extended family, and multitudes of church families. When you read *Tested and Approved,* it will be like having a personal conversation with a man who cares, loves, and is engaged with the details of life and the Kingdom. Every paragraph drips with wisdom that you know came directly from Tom's submitted life to his Father God. Pull up a chair and let the conversation begin. Your life and ministry will be activated to increased greatness.

Larry Titus
President, Kingdom Global Ministries
Apostolic Elder, Waterside Church

The road to success is paved with the wisdom of those who have traveled before us. In his newest book, *Tested and Approved,* Pastor Tom Lane beautifully captures 21 important lessons every leader must master to accomplish their God-given missions. I have had the pleasure of knowing and working in ministry with Tom for over 25 years and have seen him successfully lead both Trinity Fellowship Church and Gateway Church as Executive Pastor. His love for the Father, his submitted heart, his vast experience, and his disciplined approach to leadership give Tom the perfect perspective to craft this work. I highly recommend this book to every leader, especially the emerging leaders of this coming generation!

Jimmy Witcher
Senior Pastor, Trinity Fellowship Church
Co-author of *Kingdom Come: Living in Heaven on Earth*

There are few books we can read that truly give us insight from an individual with a lifetime of experience and learning in the ministry. Tom Lane has written just that kind of book. With decades of experience in ministry leadership in some of the largest and most influential churches in America,

Tom gives practical and insightful advice to help you navigate the difficult paths of ministry and family leadership.

Dr. Jon Chasteen
Lead Pastor, Victory Church
President, The Kings University

I was so excited when Tom told me he was writing this book. I have witnessed firsthand the fruit that these principles have produced in his life, his family, and his profession. We can all learn from his wisdom shared here.

Dr. Henry Cloud
Clinical Psychologist and Leadership Expert
New York Times Best-selling Author

I've watched Tom Lane live out the powerful lessons he shares in these 21 lessons. He gives easy-to-read, personal, and real-world nuggets of wisdom that easily translate into practical application. The principles are instantly relevant in so many areas of life and ministry, as well as business professions. It not only applies to those just stepping into ministry but also to those well into years of serving. It's a terrific compass to assess whether your leadership is on track or needs to be strengthened and stretched. This book should be required reading for every person stepping into ministry or in the midst of their season of serving. I'm grateful to have this resource for my teams.

Mallory Bassham
Executive Pastor of Multi-Campus Ministries, Gateway Church

I've been waiting for this book! Tom Lane is truly a brilliant man of God and has found a way, once again, to display his knowledge and understanding in text form. You are going to learn much, grow deeply, and be truly encouraged as you read these pages. Tom has blessed me with his teachings about being a father, and now he's doing the same by teaching us to turn to the Father. I love and appreciate the wisdom of Tom Long ... I mean Lane.

Michael Jr.
Comedian/Producer, Michael Jr. Productions

The book of Proverbs was written to transmit a lifetime of wisdom from one of the wisest men who ever lived. To me, Tom Lane is a modern-day embodiment of fatherly wisdom and a deep well of practical, godly knowledge, which I have personally been drawing from for many years. His newest book, *Tested and Approved,* is not the result of several weeks or even several months of sitting down to write a book. No, it has taken a lifetime to write it, because it is the result of a lifetime of experience. I am personally grateful for each golden chapter in this book and the life lessons they contain. For every person desiring to live a life that counts for God, this book should be on the top of your stack. It is not only *Tested and Approved,* but its message is tried and true!

Lee M. Cummings
Founding & Senior Pastor, Radiant Church
Author of *Be Radiant* and *Flourish: Planting Your Life
Where God Designed It to Thrive*

Leadership lessons are best learned in the rear-view mirror and not the windshield of life and ministry. For decades, Pastor Tom Lane has been used by God as a global Christian leader of leaders. He has led with Spirit-filled biblical humility and integrity at home, in business, and in ministry. This book has been decades in the making, and it is a must read for anyone wanting to lead like Jesus. I will be buying a stack for our staff and encouraging other pastors and leaders to do the same.

Mark Driscoll
Founding Senior Pastor, The Trinity Church
President, Mark Driscoll Ministries

Tested and Approved reflects the leadership style of its author: transparent, wise, inspiring, excellent, and authentic. It is a clear road map to unlocking an integrity-filled path to leadership success. Tom Lane's brilliant mentoring reflections and insights are a treasure chest of clearly applicable and practical principles, which are relevant and insightful to every person at every stage of their life and leadership journey.

LoriAnn V. Lowery-Biggers
CEO, BellaVaughan, Inc.
Co-Host of "The Leader's Panel" Podcast

It's been my privilege to get to know Tom Lane personally over the last few years. I've watched him from afar as he demonstrates integrity and wisdom in ministry, but I also know him up close, which gives his message even more validity. In *Tested and Approved,* Tom gives the down to earth, nuts and bolts, gritty truth about how to start strong *and* finish well. Do yourself a favor and pick up this book so you can learn from Tom's practical wisdom.

Greg Surratt
Founding Pastor, Sea Coast Church
Founding Member and President, ARC

Tom is a true spiritual father and someone I've had the privilege of getting to know for many years, both in his generous hosting of me at Gateway Church and in our partnership together in helping to lead the European Learning Communities. Throughout this time, I've been consistently blessed by Tom's amazing love, humility, and wisdom—qualities that spill over into *Tested and Approved.* This book truly contains some great life lessons. Read and be strengthened!

Dr. David Smith
Senior Pastor, KingsGate Community Church

After 30 years of pastoral ministry, I was excited to dive into *Tested and Approved,* not only because I want to grow as a leader but also because I know and so highly respect the author. Tom Lane has lived out these 21 lessons for life and ministry and has forgotten more than most of us will ever learn. Whether you've been in ministry for a long time or are just starting out, this book will greatly improve your life and leadership!

Joe Champion
Senior Pastor, Celebration Church
Lead Team Member, ARC

Tom Lane's love for life, people, and Jesus is contagious. Using real-life stories and humor, Tom draws us in and shares his wealth of leadership experience with us. The insights in this book will impact your life and your leadership.

Dr. Todd Mullins
Senior Pastor, Christ Fellowship Church
Founder, Church United

Tom Lane knows the challenges that pastors and others in full-time ministry face, and he's distilled his wisdom on overcoming those obstacles into a book you won't want to miss. *Tested and Approved* combines the instructive truth and grace of God's Word with more than 30 years of Tom's experience. The result is a passionate collection of principles sure to inspire you as well as those you serve.

Chris Hodges
Senior Pastor, Church of the Highlands
Author of *The Daniel Dilemma* and *What's Next?*

In *Tested and Approved,* Tom Lane has captured timeless principles and values of which all of us need to be reminded. These truths will help us live and minister with grace and balance in our lives as we face the challenges of time. Tom gives us tools to use as we encourage, grow, and expand our teams. No matter what season your ministry is in, Tom's 21 lessons will challenge you and grow you where you are. Stay strong in the Lord!

Thomas D. Mullins, PhD
Founding Pastor, Christ Fellowship Church
Founder, Place of Hope and Place of Hope International

Tom Lane is one of the church's greatest strategic thinkers and administrators. He has also learned a valuable lesson, one attributed to an architect from antiquity. The architect is credited with the statement: "God is in the details." These complimentary traits of deep insight and persistence in the details are two of the major reasons why Gateway Church has soared into its premier position in the nation. Tom's life embodies these traits, and in this book, he shows the rest of us a path to greatness. This is a must read for both new and seasoned leaders. Prepare to be blessed as you read these pages!

Bishop Harry Jackson
Senior Pastor, Hope Christian Church
Presiding Bishop, International Communion of Evangelical Churches

TESTED AND

APPROVED

21 LESSONS FOR
LIFE AND MINISTRY

TOM LANE

TESTED AND

APPROVED

21 LESSONS FOR
LIFE AND MINISTRY

GATEWAY®
PRESS

ISBN: 978-1-951227-24-1 Hardcover
ISBN: 978-1-951227-25-8 eBook
ISBN: 978-1-64689-156-6 Audiobook
ISBN: 978-1-951227-43-2 Companion Guide for Mentoring

We hope you hear from the Holy Spirit and receive God's richest blessings from this book
by Gateway Press. We want to provide the highest quality resources that take the messages,
music, and media of Gateway Church to the world. For more information on other resources
from Gateway Publishing®, go to gatewaypublishing.com.

Gateway Press, an imprint of Gateway Publishing
700 Blessed Way
Southlake, TX 76092
gatewaypublishing.com

Printed in the United States of America

20 21 22 23 24 — 5 4 3 2 1

TABLE OF CONTENTS

DEDICATION

WE DO NOT exist in a vacuum but in daily interactions from the learning lab called life. I am forever indebted to the people who taught, mentored, and influenced me throughout the years. There are too many to name all of them in this dedication, so I will mention those who were most influential. I am forever enriched by these great individuals!

To my wife, **Jan Frazier Lane**: I have learned so many lessons about true love, devotion, priority, and faith from you.

To my parents, **Jim and Joyce Lane**: Thank you for teaching me lessons of diligence, faithfulness, and commitment.

To my father-in-law, **Dean Frazier**: I learned the lesson of being consistent from him. He was the same person at home, at work, at church, in private, and in public. He loved God consistently in every setting of his life.

To **Pastor Elmer Murdoch**: I learned about devotion and giving lordship to Christ from him as a spiritual mentor and pastor. He taught me humble leadership, love for God's Word, service to God and people, and evangelism through a tool called "Step Up to Life."

To **Pastor Larry Titus**: You are a pastor, mentor, and friend. From you I learned lessons about structure, excellence, and the reflection of godliness as radiated from the way we live. You taught me that everything matters before God.

To **Pastor Jimmy Evans**: You are my best friend, mentor, and ministry partner. I learned lessons about friendship and ministry and the truth that obedience is better than sacrifice.

To **Pastor Robert Morris**: You are my pastor, boss, colleague, and friend. I have learned from you the power of giving God your first and your best and about the importance of asking God about everything. You taught me how to apply the simple principle of hearing, believing, and obeying to every aspect of life and ministry.

I also want to thank the staff of **Gateway Publishing** for believing in this project and walking with me to bring it to the world. Special thanks to John Andersen, Jonathan Bryce, Craig Dunnagan, Alexis Hines, Emily Jones, Kathy Krenzien, Jenny Morgan, Peyton Sepeda, and Jeremy Willis for taking this book across the finish line.

FOREWORD

MANY PEOPLE WRITE books long before they really have anything important to say. Pastor Tom has spent decades absorbing, learning, discerning, and dispensing profound spiritual insights on leadership with unmatched clarity. He has sat in boardrooms, offices, coffee shops, and on long car rides with thousands of leaders, listening and praying along the way.

Pastor Tom has earned the right to pen this book, and the Church needs to pay attention to this man, who has walked with impressive humility and courageous vision. His counsel has literally rescued churches from the abyss, healed deep chasms of broken trust, restored fallen leaders, and renewed hope in men like me.

When I first met Tom Lane in the fall of 1995, I was a wounded young man in need of help. I bore the scars of the messy, local church, and my wife, Pam, and I needed a safe community where we would be loved and heard. We needed leaders who were trustworthy and patient.

Finally, after weeks of invitations from a friend, we arrived at Trinity Fellowship in Amarillo, Texas. We were cynical but desperate. That Sunday, Pastor Tom was on the platform greeting a huge crowd of people, and each word seemed sincere and kind. He gave no performance and engaged in no hype; he simply delivered his message in clear pastoral language. I could tell he was a man who obviously loved his church.

Pastor Tom has always carried the sacred calling of a shepherd—someone who walks among and with the congregation. He eats with them, laughs with them, mourns with them, and is present with them. There's always been a bit of holy innocence about Pastor Tom, a purity of heart and motive. He was the leader I needed during that particular season of replenishing, and it's the reason I'm grateful for this book.

Most of what I've learned about leading a healthy church is modeled after Pastor Tom's life. Pam and I have watched him love Jan sincerely, father his children diligently, and serve other leaders faithfully. He was the steady force behind the supernatural growth of Gateway Church when I served there. He's been my loyal overseer since I first arrived at New Life Church. It takes a long time to become old friends, and Pastor Tom is a treasured confidant and mentor.

As you begin reading these pages, consider yourself invited to the table for a conversation with a trusted saint. Take your time to absorb these words. This wisdom was learned after a long obedience in the right direction and should be received in the same way. Listen to what has been written. Take in these words from a true spiritual father.

Brady Boyd
Senior Pastor, New Life Church
Author of *Addicted to Busy, Fear No Evil,*
and *Sons and Daughters*

INTRODUCTION

I FIRST BEGAN developing these lessons for life and ministry in 2000 when I read about Bill Gates' address entitled "11 Personalized Rules of Life," which he reportedly delivered at a high school graduation commencement. At the time, I thought he offered such good practical advice that I started personalizing some of the things I have learned from my own life and ministry so I could share them with my children and grandchildren someday. As often happens in an internet age, I later learned that Gates neither wrote nor delivered a speech like the one I had read—not to a high school and not to anyone else either. It was a little disappointing. Actually, no one even knows if he would agree with that speech. However, I do know he didn't come up with or deliver those rules.

After some time, I discovered the original text I'd read was a pared-down version of an op-ed piece penned by educational reformer Charles J. Sykes, who is best known for his book *Dumbing Down Our Kids: Why American Children Feel Good about Themselves, But Can't Read, Write, or Add*. In September 1996, *San Diego Union-Tribune* published Sykes' opinion piece.[1] Then in February 2000, an unnamed person

---

1. For further reading, see "Some Rules Kids Won't Learn in School," *San Diego Union-Tribune*, 19 September 1996.

began circulating it through email with Bill Gates as the author. That's how I first discovered it, and I have seen it a few times since. What started my thoughts in this book are really the inspiration of Charles J. Sykes rather than Bill Gates, but the list of life's lessons remains true nonetheless.

Based on that original misattributed list of lessons, I started writing my own collection of 11 pieces of guidance. As the years went by, I added additional lessons based on my experiences in life and ministry. In 2016 my friends at New Springs Church in Anderson, South Carolina, asked me to speak at a year-end staff retreat. They told me I would be one of three speakers and assigned "How to Finish Strong" as the subject of my message. At the time, I had only developed 18 of the lessons here in this book, so I wove them into my talk. I have since added three more. Thus, I now call them *21 Lessons for Life and Ministry*, which is the subtitle for this book. The title is *Tested and Approved* because I believe learning and practicing these lessons will make all of us better individuals, family leaders, and ministers.

I am certainly not suggesting these are the only lessons you will need for life and ministry. I am still learning, as are you. I expect an expanded version of this book will be released in another 20 years, or at least a sequel with the subtitle *More Lessons for Life and Ministry*. What I hope first for you is that you will read these lessons and experience some of the same feelings I did when I first read "11 Personalized Rules for Life." I am praying right now that you will gain a real advantage for your life and ministry from my experiences, both the good ones and the bad. Second, I am asking God to inspire you to sit and write your own life lessons as you learn and experience them. One day you will have the opportunity to share those lessons with the generations that follow you: your children, grand-children, and others who are watching God work through you. My greatest prayer for this book is that it will give a guideline that might shorten your learning curve.

INTRODUCTION

May God be with you on your journey as He has been with me mine. Enjoy!

But the Helper, the Holy Spirit, whom the Father will send in my name, he will teach you all things and bring to your remembrance all that I have said to you.

—John 14:26

TESTED AND

APPROVED

21 LESSONS FOR LIFE AND MINISTRY

Lesson 1

MINISTRY AND LIFE ARE NOT FAIR.

> And when those hired about the eleventh hour came, each of them received a denarius. Now when those hired first came, they thought they would receive more, but each of them also received a denarius. And on receiving it they grumbled at the master of the house, saying, *"These last worked only one hour, and you have made them equal to us who have borne the burden of the day and the scorching heat."*
> —Matthew 20:9–12, emphasis added

ONE OF THE most shocking revelations we discover about life is that *it is not fair!* Even though we know intellectually that it isn't, many people still experience internal confusion because they haven't quite accepted that fact. Have you realized and accepted it yourself? If not, I will say it again. *Life isn't fair.* And this is an absolutely true statement.

Take for instance a guy who is fit as a fiddle. He runs, hangs out at the gym, eats mostly healthy foods, and sleeps the recommended number of hours. Then he discovers he has high blood pressure, clogged arteries, and heart disease. And to add insult to everything else, he dies at an early age.

Now compare his lifestyle to another guy who never exercises but eats without concern for his health, consuming unlimited carbohydrates and ordering dessert at every meal (with junk food snacks in between). At his annual physical, the doctor says he's in "perfect health." His blood pressure is normal, his heartbeats are regular and strong, and his arteries look like they have been cleaned with a plumber's snake. This guy lives to be over 100 years old.

What?! No fair!

The issue of fairness rises to another level when we consider life in ministry. I hate to lead you into disillusionment or burst your bubble, but ministry parallels life—and *ministry is not fair either*. Consider the pastor who has not received the same level of training as you, doesn't present himself as well as you, isn't in as affluent an area as you, and hasn't spent the same number of years in ministry as you. You, on the other hand, may have a seminary education with other advanced training. You always present yourself with the appropriate dignity expected of a pastor, and you planted your church in one of the most strategic demographic areas of the city. However, your church is struggling with attendance, finances, or maybe both while this other pastor has a successful megachurch.

Ministry parallels life—and *ministry is not fair either*.

Neither life nor ministry are based on fairness, and if you focus on fairness, neither one will ever make sense to you. You'll be disappointed, frustrated, and eventually cynical. Life must be based on faith no matter what you do, ministry or otherwise. Begin with this most basic understanding: *God is your Creator.* Not only that, but He is also good and has a plan, purpose, and role for you to fill. That is true for all of us who have been called by Him (Romans 8:28).

In one of my business classes in college, the professor gave an assignment to a group of us to replicate a research study on entrepreneurial success. We were told to identify the components of success as it relates to business. Through this exercise, we discovered our findings were identical to the study we modeled. We observed factors such as financial success, sales growth, and organizational size to measure the success of selected businesses. What we discovered is "luck" (or providence for those of us who are Christians) and skillful effort played relatively equal roles in predicting a business's success. That discovery was a little unsettling for me as a young business student.

Numerous times in my years at Gateway Church, pastors of other churches have asked me to reveal the "secret sauce" of Gateway's success. The answer does not rest on our luck, skill, or top-secret ministry formula. The reason is *God*. He is the secret to our success, but it's not a secret we want to keep to ourselves. His plans, purpose, and sovereign work are the most significant factors that have led to any triumph we have experienced. The answer I give is not intended to be flippant; I really believe it. However, some pastors look at me with a mixture of disappointment, dissatisfaction, and even suspicion. From the way I interpret their facial expressions, it appears as if they think I am protecting a tightly held trade secret or withholding the whole truth to keep them from experiencing what we have at Gateway Church.

Then I will point those who are curious to some of the practical things Gateway Church does that I think are important for reaching a new level of success. In truth, however, no other church can simply attempt to replicate the things we do and expect the same ministry results. So I go back to what I said originally: God is the one who directs and anoints our efforts to produce His purpose and results. I don't have another truth to offer. He has done something by His own purpose and design that is unique to Gateway Church, and He is working to do something unique and amazing in other churches—but only if they will hear, believe, and obey what He says to do. Focus your attention and efforts on listening to the Holy Spirit and then, by all godly means, follow what He reveals to you.

God is the one who directs and anoints our efforts to produce His purpose and results.

Since the local church is really a mirror of the family, this truth applies equally to your family. Are you looking with hidden jealousy at another family and thinking, *No fair! We do more for the church than they do. We love each other and demonstrate it more than they do. We love God and demonstrate our love for Him as much or more than they do. So why isn't our family blessed like theirs?*

Now, I know that doesn't seem fair, and from a human perspective, it may not be fair. However, the determination of "fairness" really isn't up to us. If that makes someone uncomfortable, then they need to take it up with God. He is the one who determined long ago that real life and success would be about faith—trust and reliance on His nature and character—which will give us contentment with His assignment for our lives and ministries. That kind of faith will enable you to fulfill His purpose in your life, I promise. It will allow you to trust His heart when faith is not yet sight and His hand still seems invisible.

Pause for a moment here and read carefully: I am not giving you an excuse to become lazy. God has His part, but you also have yours. As the old saying goes, God can miraculously move mountains, but sometimes He will do it with you and a shovel. You must remain diligent if you want to know and understand what He wants for you. Then you will have to move with courage and diligence to follow your new understanding of His assignment and act to the best of your abilities.

Give up the bad habit of trying to compare yourself, your ministry, or your circumstances to someone else's. That toxic thinking will lead you to a place you don't need to go. In fact, comparison can only lead you to one of two unhealthy extremes—depression or pride. Don't let the seeds of arrogance and pride find fertile soil in your eyes, mind, or heart. Turn away from insecurity, self-doubt, and self-hate; they will only become barriers that keep you from fulfilling God's assignment for you.

You know God is in charge, right? He is the King, and He has His Kingdom. He will rule and guide it as He sees fit. He doesn't respond to orders or democratic mandates that make the majority happy. But He is a good, kind, compassionate, and loving King who wants the best for you. From His essential goodness, He is ultimately and absolutely fair, and His definition of "fairness" is the only one that counts.

God your Father knows exactly what is best for you, far more than you know yourself. Rest in that truth. When you become frustrated by what seems to be unfair, ask yourself what the source of your frustration is. Make sure it is not comparison, which is reflected in the idea that you deserve or are entitled to fairness because of all your efforts and hard work. In God's eyes, all of us are simply His humble servants, and He wants us to seek and find His good will.

If fairness is the most important thought in your mind, I will tell you what I used to tell my children: there is only one fair in Texas, and it happens once in the fall. Ask yourself, *Am I seeking fairness, or am I nurturing faith?* Expecting fairness will lead you down the dark paths of comparison and expectation, but faith will lead you to light and life. It will ultimately take you to the place where you will hear, "Well done, my good and faithful servant! Enter into the joy of your master!"

His master said to him, "Well done, good and faithful servant. You have been faithful over a little; I will set you over much. Enter into the joy of your master."

—Matthew 25:23

Lesson 2

MINISTRY IS ABOUT PEOPLE BEFORE IT IS ABOUT RESULTS.

By this all people will know that you are my disciples, if you have love for one another.

—John 13:35

If anyone says, "I love God," and hates his brother, he is a liar; for he who does not love his brother whom he has seen cannot love God whom he has not seen. And this commandment we have from him: whoever loves God must also love his brother.

—1 John 4:20–21

WHEN I WAS in college, my dad and his business partners purchased 11 warehouse properties from a wholesale paper distribution chain. Before that time, he and his colleagues were employees for this same company their entire working lives. I admired my dad and his success as a business leader, and I wanted to follow his footsteps into business. Ultimately, if God would allow me, I wanted to run his company.

One day my dad and I were talking about business, and he posed a question to me. He asked, "What business do you think I am in?" I suspected this was a trick question because he surely knew I was aware that he was in the wholesale paper distribution business. I cautiously answered, "I'm not exactly sure, but

I think it's the paper business." Then he responded, "Well, that is what would appear to be the right answer as it is the obvious answer, but it's not exactly right. I am in the *people* business."

My dad continued by telling me that he managed people (his employees) in the organization to achieve a result. He told me he built relationships with customers to win their favor and earn their trust so they would purchase our products and we could service their needs. My dad also told me how he managed the expectations of investors and bankers as part of his responsibilities in the organization. Managing and relating to all these people culminated in the sale of paper products. Finally, my dad said that by doing these things consistently over a long time period with a servant heart devoted to helping people with their needs, he gained personal fulfillment, which then translated into his success. He was teaching me through this question and subsequent interactions how to serve and care for people regardless of my chosen field of work.

One of the most consistent truths I have heard from Pastor Robert Morris is that every person is "called" by God. He explains that some fill individual jobs, such as doctors, lawyers, plumbers, social workers, or service employees, but God "calls" all of us to love people and represent Him in a life of service devoted to Him.

Often, we hear people define the "call" to ministry service too narrowly. We use that term almost exclusively to refer to God directing an individual into vocational ministry. I find it incredibly significant that my dad looked at his company first as a "people" business rather than a "paper" business. As Pastor Robert would say, God "calls" each of us into a place of service regardless of the particular industry. My dad's "call" to the people business brought about phenomenal sales results for the company's paper products, but even more importantly, it provided him a platform of influence and service to hundreds and maybe thousands of people. And if we follow his example, we will allow God's light to shine brightly from our lives for all to see.

God "calls" each of us into a place of service regardless of the particular industry.

My dad's approach to business and Pastor Robert's approach to ministry have helped me relate to business leaders in our congregation. When we put people first, it reorients our thinking and helps us recognize the dignity of each person's work. This way of thinking leads us to affirm God's call on every person's life as something significant regardless of their vocation.

When you carry this broader perspective of God's call, your ministry impact will increase because your pastoral heart will be more empathetic and your pastoral voice more persuasive. It will give you a new ability to encourage people to listen to God's voice and follow what He tells them to do in their businesses as an extension of His call on their lives. You will be able to motivate them to faithful and diligent work, and their reputation, influence, and impact will grow with their customers, employees, colleagues, and peers. This is their slice of the "people business" under their heavenly Father's leadership.

We have raised people up at Gateway Church with a ministry perspective—*we are in the people business.* We sincerely believe this is the foundation on which healthy ministry is built. We recognize the fundamental difference between ministry thinking as opposed to secular business thinking. It may seem like a small variance or even like a play on words, yet it really is important. A business mindset focuses on producing results and sees people as one of the resources to bring about those results. On the other hand, a ministry mindset looks at people as the ultimate result God wants to produce. People are God's living stones; He is using them to build a place where His good works will be displayed for all to see and consequently glorify Him. Changing your mindset will radically alter the way you build, manage, and maintain relationships and your ministry.

In both ministry and secular business approaches, people are needed, but other than that, there are glaring differences. When product and profit are the focus, people are consumed to get the result. When people are the focus, programs and resources are consumed to get the result. Recognizing the difference between these two approaches will radically change the way you treat people and lead them in your organization.

In a secular business, financial results are the focus. Efficiently producing a product and selling it at a targeted profit margin is the reason these types of businesses exist, or so some would say. When a business profitably produces a product, it is through a process that builds relationships with employees, vendors, and customers. A business might build a particularly close relationship with a valued customer or a key vendor, but it will be maintained with the goal of producing that profitable result. When the product becomes obsolete or profitability slows, the customer or vendor relationship will disappear as well. A social friendship may last beyond the product, but the relationship qualitatively changes.

In a healthy ministry, relationships are maintained with an eternal perspective. That kind of ministry builds relationships with those who share a similar heart and motivation and then join with the ministry as financial partners and volunteers to serve people and accomplish common goals. The very nature of ministry means we want to affect people's lives. To effectively minister to people, we must develop and maintain relationships with them. It takes a foundation of trust to meet the ministry needs of an individual, and then trust grows based on that relationship. The relationships we form in ministry are with church members, church attendees, volunteers, or those individuals who are helped as part of the ministry's outreach to the community. The depth of the individual relationships we develop is what will draw people into the ministry. Why is this true? *Because people don't care how much you know until they know how much you care.*

There are some business leaders and owners who have embraced this revelation for their businesses. In doing so, they make people more important than profit, and relationships serve as the foundation for building their businesses. Through this similarity, the call to business and the call to vocational ministry have the same formula for success.

We make relationships a priority because that is what God does. He put His relationship with us first when He chose His strategy for our redemption. According to His plan, God sent His Son to repair the broken relationship between us and our Father. Once our relationship with Him was restored through the cross, He then began to unfold ministry in our lives. God will not force ministry upon us; rather, He offers us ministry through our restored relationship. If we force people to accept the results that we want for them but violate their wills in the process, then we do not represent God's heart. Nor do we satisfy His standard of love.

Love never gives up.
Love cares more for others than for self.
Love doesn't want what it doesn't have.
Love doesn't strut,
Doesn't have a swelled head,
Doesn't force itself on others,
Isn't always "me first,"
Doesn't fly off the handle,

Doesn't keep score of the sins of others,
Doesn't revel when others grovel,
Takes pleasure in the flowering of truth,
Puts up with anything,
Trusts God always,
Always looks for the best,
Never looks back,
But keeps going to the end (1 Corinthians 13:4–7 MSG).

As you think about your vocation, imagine God asking, "What business do you think you are in?" You might think it is the salvation business, or the deliverance business, or the discipleship business, or the business of worship by which we soak in His presence. You might think it's a sales business, manufacturing business, or a retail business. You are not wrong to conclude from your observation that those things are produced in the process of your efforts in people's lives. However, those fantastic benefits, as significant as they are, are only some of the by-products that come from a ministry or business that is "All About People." Why is this so? Because first, before anything else, our Father is in the people business.

Ask yourself, *Do I ever become focused on producing a result at the expense of people?* Do you ever think fulfilling God's "call" for your life is more important than your children, your marriage, or your other relationships? Do you sometimes think God will be pleased if you have produced a string of successful business or ministry results, yet you have left broken relationships in your wake? If any of these are true for you, then it's time to adjust your thinking. Results without relationships are just noisy, busy activity that really amounts to nothing. Generosity and sacrifice not motivated by and connected to relationships may make you feel good or even make you a lot of money in the present, but in the end, they amount to nothing.

Results without relationships are just noisy, busy activity that really amounts to nothing.

Remember, your heavenly Father is in the people business!

If I speak in the tongues of men and of angels, but have not love, I am a noisy gong or a clanging cymbal. And if I have prophetic powers, and understand all mysteries and all knowledge, and if I have all faith, so as to remove mountains, but have not love, I am nothing. If I give away all I have, and if I deliver up my body to be burned, but have not love, I gain nothing.

—1 Corinthians 13:1–3

Lesson 3

WE WILL BE KNOWN
BY THE FRUIT WE PRODUCE.

So, *every healthy tree bears good fruit, but the diseased tree bears bad fruit.* A healthy tree cannot bear bad fruit, nor can a diseased tree bear good fruit. Every tree that does not bear good fruit is cut down and thrown into the fire. Thus you will recognize them by their fruits.

—Matthew 7:17–20, emphasis added

In the same way, let your light shine before others, so that they may see your good works and give glory to your Father who is in heaven.

—Matthew 5:16

WHEN I WAS growing up, my parents instilled in me the importance of keeping a good name. Sometimes when they told me I wasn't allowed to do something, they would say, "We are Lanes, and the Lanes are not going to participate in that behavior or act that way." It did not matter to them that my friends' parents were letting them do something. My parents' perspective was always to consider and protect the Lane name.

You may have had this experience, even as an adult. Sometimes other people, including your friends, will encourage you to participate in an activity or to act in a certain way that you know does not and will not contribute to giving you a good name. You know that activity isn't right, nor is it in good taste, but your friends tell you it will be "okay" anyway. They may even try to influence you to join them by saying, "Everyone is doing it!" Still, you know it is not okay. In fact, you know it will very likely return to you in a most unexpected way over time and threaten your reputation.

As believers, our lives are supposed to bear fruit. This fruit will often take the form of our "good name" or our "good deeds" done to benefit others. When we demonstrate integrity and consistent behavior, our influence grows, and others take note. Just as we plant and grow crops to eat, the quantity, quality, and size of the fruit produced in our lives will be determined by the things we do. Every farmer knows that a fruitful harvest is determined by the fertilizer, water, sunlight, climate, soil, and careful cultivation the land receives. Smart parents similarly know that their diligent care to mentor, correct, and encourage their children will determine the fruit produced in their children's lives as they mature. God is a partner to both farmers and parents and will supply everything they need to grow and produce fruit in its season. Both farmers and parents know that even with diligent effort a portion of the potential fruitfulness of their harvest rests outside their own hands. Weather's elements affect the farmer's harvest. Likewise, the company our children keep affects the fruitful harvest in their lives. That is why parents must remain diligent and proactive, just like the farmer, to make sure "bugs" don't infest the crop and negatively impact the harvest of fruit in their children's lives.

Jesus' followers are expected to produce good fruit in heat and drought just as well as they do in good weather and plentiful rain. As children of our Father, we are His trees planted by living waters (see Psalm 1). Your Father expects you to be hearty and healthy so you can bring forth good fruit regardless of the situation. Your friends, extended family, and the rest of the world may be oblivious to your difficult circumstances, yet the fruit your life yields will always be evident for all to see. People will critically evaluate your life to see if your values and what is advertised through your name's reputation match the fruit you produce. Even though some of these evaluations will be demanding, unrealistic, or even legalistic, if you don't measure up to the values and faith you profess, then people will criticize you, discard you, and move on.

God will not be as harsh with His judgments, as long as you remain connected to Him. He will work with you to help you produce fruit in every season and in every weather circumstance you may encounter. Many people in the world will expect you to accomplish something *before* they will allow you to enjoy the satisfaction of achievement. They may even try to suppress or rob you of that satisfaction, all the while demanding that you accomplish more. Meanwhile, they will tell you that they are helping you through their criticism and demands, which they believe will keep you from pride and arrogance. When you feel pressured by others' demands, remember that God is the only one who valued you before you did a single thing. He is the one who rejoices over you and celebrates every incremental milestone of your progress.

When I prayed to receive Christ as my Savior, I also received Him as my Lord. I was told that doing so meant He was in charge and I was no longer the ruler of my life. I was stepping off the throne of my life and giving Him His rightful place as my Lord. That awareness has guided my life and ministry for decades. In all things, I desire to know and do His will. The day I put my eyes on Him, He became the focus of my desire and the expression of my purpose. That decision made it easy to understand the model of ministry that God will bless. This is the model I have taught and used in my various roles in ministry: *God is the focus, people are the beneficiaries, and everything else is just a tool for the service of God and people.*

When you feel pressured by others' demands, remember that God is the only one who valued you before you did a single thing.

I want the fruit of my life to reflect my devotion to God in all I do. I want to reflect a genuine intimacy with Him and then for that relationship to serve as my motivation, which drives my desire to help others. I want to inspire believers to follow the same path. Together, I want us to advance the work of God's Kingdom on earth just as it is done in heaven. I want my values to be His values. I want Him to direct my pursuits. When people evaluate my life, I want them to glorify God because of His fruit that they see in me. To the extent that they see anything they would desire for themselves, I want it to be the substance of God—His Word, His character, His presence, and His work reflected in my life. That is the fruit of a "good name" I want to establish and protect.

What fruit is your life producing? What kind of name do you have in your industry, community, and among your family members and friends? Do you know that God is inspecting the fruit your life is producing? Is it fruit of anger, selfishness, materialism, and self-promotion? Or is it fruit of generosity, compassion, faithfulness, and diligence? Do your reputation and influence reflect God's work and presence in your life?

I encourage you to settle for nothing less than the fruit of His presence. Ask God to work in you to produce His fruit in your character, your thoughts, your marriage, your leadership, and every other area of your life. Right now, ask the Holy Spirit to help you bear the fruit of His good name, and He will! Remember this: we are the sons and daughters of the living God. Make sure you represent Him well with your name and the influence of your life so you will bear fruit for His glory!

> A good name is to be chosen rather than great riches,
>   and favor is better than silver or gold.
>   —Proverbs 22:1

Lesson 4

SUCCESS IS A PROCESS.

This Book of the Law shall not depart from your mouth, but you shall meditate on it day and night, so that you may be careful to do according to all that is written in it. For then you will make your way prosperous, and then you will have good success.

—Joshua 1:8

For what does it profit a man to gain the whole world and forfeit his soul?

—Mark 8:36

As FAR BACK as I can remember, I always wanted to succeed. I pursued success in everything I did. It didn't matter if I was engaged in athletics, friendships, school, or eventually a career. No matter what I was doing, I wanted to be good at it. Today, I know success is a process that requires diligence, faithfulness, hard work, humility, selfless service, and obedience to God's direction. Success also involves failures that teach us what not to do and reorient us in the right direction according to God's path. Success doesn't happen by accident; it takes time and perseverance. God established principles to help us in every situation we face, and when we follow them, they produce success. You need to hear this: you will *not* start at the top in any of your endeavors, nor will you produce great results without diligence. Success won't come easily, but it is attainable.

When I reached my teens and started thinking seriously about a career, I looked at my dad as the model to follow. I thought of him as a successful man. He started working for his company right out of college, and his first position was in the warehouse. Over time, he moved up to sales and management, and he eventually became one of the principle owners of the company. My dad accomplished all these things without compromising his marriage, family, or friends, and I wanted to pattern my life after his.

As I examined his path toward success, I compared it against others who had followed a different direction. Some of those people made a lot of money and even advanced in their careers, but at the expense of their health, their families, their reputations, or their friends. Ironically, the more assets, titles, and positions they accumulated, the more heartbreak they had as well. Surely that couldn't be the right pattern for success!

After I made a commitment to follow Christ, I discovered that the true foundation of success is to know and do the will of God. By that, I mean He wants us to fulfill His desires in a way that represents His character. We can focus our lives on His will and rest in the reality that He has good plans for us; to give us peace and prosper us (Jeremiah 29:11). I made it a goal to conduct myself and my business in a way that honored God and responded to His leading and direction. I witnessed some people who were so focused on position, title, income, and the accumulation of things as their measures of success that they gave no consideration to God's will in the process. They would take any path that would get them where they wanted to go. They were busy building their lives without considering that they had shaky foundations underneath.

Without giving regard to God or His principles, these people were building on dangerously unstable ground. As I watched them, I realized their relationships with God were nonexistent.

At best, they would tip their hat to Him once a week and reluctantly attend a church service. In many cases, they only thought of God for that one hour they sat in the pew, and that was if they considered Him at all. They recognized their duty to family, community, or even God to fulfill their weekly church obligations, but once they were done, they were off again to pursue their path to success in the quickest way with any means at their disposal.

The true foundation of success is to know and do the will of God.

I really wish I could say that I have never seen anyone in vocational ministry veer down that destructive path, but sadly, I can't. I have watched people in ministry pursue success with the same misguided intensity as those in secular business careers. Even worse, those in vocational ministry are tempted to drive themselves with the wrong idea that God expects them to grow a big church, fulfill a great vision, and establish their influence—all as a means to make a big splash for God. They proceed by any method they feel will accomplish these things the fastest. The only difference between them and their secular business counterparts is that the former put God's name on it and use Him to justify their misbehavior.

It doesn't matter whether someone is in vocational ministry or has a career in business. The mindset of "succeed at all costs" has the same high price. It will cost the things that matter most, including health, family, reputation, and friends.

The Bible has only one definition for success—the obedient fulfillment of God's will and desires. This is a short, simple statement, but it can become cloudy and vague in its application when personal desires and peer pressures encourage us to take matters into our own hands, deluding us into thinking we are the authors of our own success.

Some people believe in the statement, "God helps those who help themselves." This familiar quotation reflects the idea that God leaves it completely up to us to pursue our own success. In my experience, this is a false and dangerous assumption to embrace. It reflects only part of our partnership with God. He does expect us to act rather than become passive while we sit and wait for Him to act. Nevertheless, we should act in response to God's leading as we are obedient to His voice. He neither wants nor expects us to operate independently from His direction and work.

In 1 Samuel 15 King Saul camped with his army at Gilgal. God's prophet Samuel had told Saul to battle against the Amalekites, and when the Israelite army won, they were to destroy the Amalekite army completely, including all their animals and property. Samuel told Saul that God's command was to spare no one and take none of their property as a battle prize. Saul and his troops engaged in the fight, and God aided them in their victory. However, Saul followed only part of God's commands that Samuel had delivered. He took matters into his own hands, sparing the life of the Amalekite king, Agag, and keeping the best of the property the soldiers captured in battle. Saul abandoned obedience because of "fear of men" and pressure from his leaders and soldiers.

After the battle, Samuel arrived on the scene, and Saul eagerly greeted him with jubilation over the Israelites' victory. Samuel, however, was not pleased. Through God's commands, Saul knew what he was supposed to do, yet he had not obeyed. Saul's joy quickly turned into bitter regret because that day, God rejected him as king.

Success is not the result of your brilliance, strategic efforts, or individual diligence; rather, it comes by the grace and mercy of God, who works in and through you. If you define success by your accumulation of wealth or your victory over your competition, then you totally miss God's definition of success. Solomon wrote,

> There is an evil that I have seen under the sun, and it lies heavy on mankind: a man to whom God gives wealth, possessions, and honor, so that he lacks nothing of all that he desires, yet God does not give him power to enjoy them, but a stranger enjoys them. This is vanity; it is a grievous evil (Ecclesiastes 6:1–2).

It is true that you need diligence, faithfulness, and hard work to produce the fruit of success. However, only when you link those important qualities to your obedience to God's direction will they lead you to the success God intends for you. God's success will be followed by contentment and thankfulness.

Solomon continued,

> Everyone also to whom God has given wealth and possessions and power to enjoy them, *and to accept his lot and rejoice in his toil*—this is the gift of God (Ecclesiastes 5:19, emphasis added).

In God's eyes success comes as a result of your obedient actions linked with your individual efforts. That is the process by which God will make the most of the talents and resources He has graciously given to you. If you try to define success in any other way, then you will fall into the devil's trap, and he will rob you of the joy of God's blessings and partnership.

Ask yourself, *Am I pursuing success as defined by a standard other than God's? Am I comparing my results with others as a measure of success?* Don't measure your success by comparing yourself to someone else. God is your standard as you pursue

His plan and direction. Obediently follow Him with diligence as you apply your talents and resources to the process. Only then will you discover and fulfill God's will in all things.

God reveals His measure of success in this statement: "Well done, good and faithful servant!" (Matthew 25:21, 23). Press on in your pursuit. Don't allow yourself to become distracted, discouraged, or disillusioned in your efforts. Make sure you are building your success on obedience to His will for you. God measures our success by our obedience. As you obediently fulfill His assignment for your life, you will discover your true success.

God measures our success by our obedience.

Whoever is slothful will not roast his game,
  but the diligent man will get precious wealth.
                                        —Proverbs 12:27

Lesson 5

ACCOUNTABILITY IS
A GOOD THING.

Likewise, you who are younger, *be subject to the elders*. Clothe yourselves, all of you, with humility toward one another, for "God opposes the proud but gives grace to the humble." Humble yourselves, therefore, under the mighty hand of God so that at the proper time he may exalt you, casting all your anxieties on him, because he cares for you. Be sober-minded; be watchful. Your adversary the devil prowls around like a roaring lion, seeking someone to devour.

—1 Peter 5:5–8, emphasis added

Let every person *be subject to the governing authorities*. For there is no authority except from God, and those that exist have been instituted by God. Therefore whoever resists the authorities resists what God has appointed, and those who resist will incur judgment.

—Romans 13:1–2, emphasis added

If anyone says, "I love God," and hates his brother, he is a liar; for he who does not love his brother whom he has seen cannot love God whom he has not seen. And this commandment we have from him: whoever loves God must also love his brother.

—1 John 4:20–21

WHAT DOES IT mean to be "under authority"? Could I be under authority yet not be accountable for my actions, behavior, or the fruitfulness of my life? Could we say we are under God's authority and accountable to Him but then live as we please, accountable to no one? How do we passionately pursue God's purposes while still living within the boundaries of accountability? These questions need answers because they will ultimately determine whether we will fulfill God's purposes in our lives. They will shape the platform of our influence for Him. God expects accountability in all aspects of our lives and in every stage of our development.

God expects accountability in all aspects of our lives and in every stage of our development.

I played varsity football when I was in high school. I have to say it was American football, because readers everywhere else in the world use the word "football" to mean what we in the US call "soccer." I was a starter in both my junior and senior years, which means my coaches considered me one of the better players on the team along with the other starters. In my senior year, just as the season began, our coaches required team practice twice a day. We called them "two-a-days." For some unexplainable reason, the skills I had as a sophomore and junior seemed to no longer be with me. Every practice my coach seemed increasingly frustrated with me. After several days of his focused correction (and not the kind or sensitive type), I once again missed a blocking assignment in a scrimmage. So I left the field and told my backup to take my place.

However, my backup messed up like I had and missed his blocking assignment. At first, the coach thought it was still me on the field, so he started yelling at my replacement: "Lane!" Then he paused for a moment and yelled, "You're not Lane. Where is Lane? Lane, get over here!" There I was, standing on the sidelines feeling sorry for myself. When I trotted over to my coach, he grabbed my helmet's faceguard and shook it as he lectured me. He loudly explained that I had no business taking myself off the field without his direction.

Next, he asked me a most poignant question, although I didn't see it that way at the time. "Lane," he shouted, "do you think you can do a better job of coaching than me?" I responded timidly, "Uh no ... no, sir." I had the right answer, but it didn't change his emotions. He was upset because I had taken matters into my own hands. There I was, thinking he was going to shake my head off with his nose inches away from mine as he reinforced his extremely valid point. I don't know about all other sports, but American football coaches aren't paid to be polite. Once he finished reminding me at the top of his lungs that he was the coach and I was the player, he shoved me toward the huddle on the field and told me never to take myself out of action again unless I was specifically instructed by a coach to do so. I can confidently say that I never did that again, regardless of how poorly I thought I was playing.

When you're a player on a team, you are accountable to do your job, first to your coaches and then to all the other team members. You're not a free and independent agent—you gave up that option when you joined the team. It's no longer up to you to determine if you're needed or not. You no longer get to decide if someone else can fill your role better than you can. You are now responsible to do your best to fulfill your assignment, to listen to and learn from your coach, and to execute his game plan.

I am fully aware that we live in an age of independence. People define freedom as an individual's right to be unencumbered by either oversight or accountability. But is that God's view of freedom? Not according to the Bible. We can only experience freedom as God intended for us in the context of accountability and oversight. All individuals are accountable to God whether they acknowledge it or not.

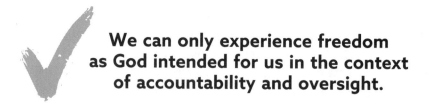

We can only experience freedom as God intended for us in the context of accountability and oversight.

God created all things and continues to own them. When human beings foolishly sinned and stepped away from God's ownership, He purchased them back through the sacrifice of Jesus Christ on the cross. God manifests His call for accountability in our lives through the human authority under which He places us. Your authorities can be your boss, a police officer, a pastor, or any governmental official. When your life began, God placed you under the authority of your parents.

Every person will ultimately acknowledge accountability to God and the institutions He established, either by choice during this lifetime or by His strong hand at the end of the age when He will call all of us to give an account of our lives. I encourage you to be wise and not resist it; rather, embrace it now by choice and live under accountability in every arena of your life. God intended for oversight to be relational, engaged, and caring. He does not want it to be harsh or controlling but kind and generous as an extension of the way He acts.

You may feel as though those in authority over you are unjust or incompetent. God has ways of dealing with those who don't represent Him or who even actively misrepresent Him. Leaders who abuse their positions of authority will have to give an account to God. Every leader in authority should understand that education, experience, and hard work may be some of the factors that contributed to their individual successes, but God is the one who puts people in places of authority. If they fail to recognize this fact, then they will have great regret on the day when everyone will be called to give an account.

Regardless of the ladder rung of authority on which you stand, you are still under authority and expected to be accountable. Therefore, as people who are under authority, we must do what is right before God regardless of what others are doing. Sometimes that will mean tolerating something that is neither just nor fair as it applies to us. Ungodly leadership oversight does not justify resistance or rebellion.

I realize that you may have objections to this way of thinking, especially if someone in authority has hurt or mistreated you. However, don't use those experiences to justify independent and rebellious actions that will put you in opposition to God. When Saul took actions that were not right and later defended them to Samuel, the prophet responded,

> Has the Lord *as great* delight in burnt offerings and sacrifices,
> As in obeying the voice of the Lord?
> Behold, to obey is better than sacrifice,
> *And* to heed than the fat of rams.
> For rebellion *is as* the sin of witchcraft,
> And stubbornness *is as* iniquity and idolatry.
> Because you have rejected the word of the Lord,
> He also has rejected you from *being* king (1 Samuel 15:22–23).

Samuel said this because Saul had acted independently and had put himself at odds with God. Does this story seem harsh to you? I understand how someone might think that but only if you minimize the importance of obedience and accountability. You don't want to be in Saul's position.

Some will defend their own behaviors by asking if I am saying believers during World War II should have submitted to ungodly Nazi leadership. Am I saying a person who is being abused physically, emotionally, or spiritually should submit to the abuse of someone in authority over them? I am aware of these types of questions and that these circumstances sometimes exist, so let me be clear: *no,* I am not saying God requires us to submit to *all* authority. If someone in authority orders you to do something illegal, immoral, or unethical, then you must take a stand for God's values. Submission is always first to God. There is an order of priority even as we submit to the authorities He has placed over us. God does not expect blind submission. His higher calling means that we surrender first to Him, which may put us at odds with those in authority.

However, we should not use God as our excuse to ignore the requirements of submission to authority simply because we don't want to follow directions. I recognize my own tendency to adopt this tactic, and I have seen it in others as well. We have an incredible ability to disapprove of any leadership directives we dislike or disagree with and then call them abusive, unethical, or immoral. By labeling them as such, we think our judgment gives us the right to resist or even instigate outright rebellion. When we justify ourselves in this way, we bring God into the equation, thinking we are acting under His authority, which then gives us the right to resist and rebel. But the truth is that we don't like what our authorities are asking us to do. Perhaps they did not ask with appropriate kindness or politeness in their tone. They may not have been sensitive to our circumstances or emotions. Or the situation might be that we simply don't want to do what they are asking us to do, so we judge it to be "wrong," which helps us to justify our resistance, independence, and rebellion. Even more damning is that we say (and may even sincerely believe) that God gave us the license to move in that direction.

We should not use God as our excuse to ignore the requirements of submission to authority simply because we don't want to follow directions.

Have you ever noticed this tendency in yourself? If you haven't, then it might be because you're not looking close enough! Our fleshly and carnal natures operate this way in each one of us. We must resist our flesh and submit to God through the authorities He puts in our lives. That means we must actively choose to surrender and submit. Under God, we are responsible to build positive relationships with the authorities God has put us under, which means we are willing to receive their direction and correction. Their responsibility is to inspect, direct, and correct us as together we jointly seek God's plan for us.

In school, you may have thought your teacher was tough, and some truly are. But wait until you get a job with a boss. Every boss and every teacher are different. Some have more relational awareness than others. Good bosses have an awareness of those with whom they work. These are the kinds of relational leaders who teach, coach, and mentor even while they are producing positive results. However, not all bosses have relational awareness. Some of them are so focused on producing results that they are insensitive to feelings, or even worse, they don't care how their directives emotionally impact their employees.

I would remind you not to wear your feelings on your shirt-sleeves, which means don't become so sensitive that it will hinder your ability to perform as a good employee. If you feel you are under the oversight of someone who is harsh or unfair, then *pray.* God is the one who establishes all authority, and through prayer, He will change you or your boss. The transformation may not happen immediately, but He is working through your prayers to change your attitude, move you to another situation, or even remove your boss.

Godly and intelligent authority will build people, and in the process, it will build a team to help accomplish the necessary work. Not all authority is godly, but God will use all authority, whether good or evil, to accomplish His purposes in our lives. Of course, His ultimate purposes are for our eternal good. Never lose sight of this fact as you responsibly walk in accountability.

Submission to authority means that you will surrender yourself and your talents to the guidance and leadership of another person. You collaborate with a team to produce excellent results. How you respond to authority matters because your attitude influences your behavior, whether you think it does or not. You will affect and infect those around you, for good or bad. That is why submission is first a heart issue, because attitudes flow from your heart.

By what process should you walk in accountability? There are two very important steps:

- *First, make a list of the people to whom you are willing to submit.* Hopefully, your boss will be one of those. Then you can expand your list to your mentors, which means other mature believers who love God and love you. They are the ones who are willing to tell you the truth rather than what you want to hear. If you do not have people like this speaking into your life, checking your attitudes, and confirming the direction of your decisions, then you can't claim to be submitted and accountable yet.

- *Second, before you act on an idea or a leading you believe is from God, submit it these people.* Wait for their input, confirmation, and approval before moving forward. If you act independently on your own initiative and seek forgiveness after the fact rather than permission before you go, then you still can't claim to be submitted and accountable.

Early in my pastoral ministry career, I had to learn these lessons. A new year began, and our church had purchased a Quonset hut that had once been a roller skating rink with the intent of converting it into our youth building. Once the construction began, the process took longer and cost more than we had planned. One day, my senior pastor and best friend, Jimmy Evans, approached me and said, "Tom, we have to wrap this project up because it is taking too long and costing too much." I replied, "I agree." On that same day, the project manager who was also on our staff told me that in order to get a permit to operate the café we had drawn into the building plans, we needed a grease trap for a sewer line outside the building. I asked him how much it would cost, and he answered, "Twenty-five thousand dollars." I told him to proceed but to do that and no more. I also stressed to him that we needed to bring the project to a close, to which he agreed. As the construction crew continued working on the building, Jimmy drove by. He observed the additional work and immediately called me on the phone to ask what was happening. I explained the situation, and he said, "Okay, do that and no more!" I acknowledged his instructions and said, "I got it. No more."

My attitude wasn't good, even though I responded in the right way. After the installation of the grease trap, the project manager approached me and said, "We have another problem." I exclaimed, "Now what?!" He replied, "We are ready to install the tables in the café. Some of the tables line the walls and need to be attached, but we have no backing in the walls to secure them. If we attach them to the drywall without some type of support, then they won't hold up under the pressure of daily use. They will quickly and easily pull out of the wall." I sighed and then asked, "So how much will that cost?" And he responded, "It should be around three thousand dollars to add the wainscot paneling around the walls so the tables can be securely installed." I said, "Okay, do that and no more!"

Later that afternoon, some members of the pastoral staff met to play basketball at the new youth building while the finish work was underway in the café. As I came into the locker room to change for the game, Jimmy met me with the same question he asked before: "Tom, *what* is going on? Do they not understand what *wrap it up* means?" Once again, I explained the cause of the additional work and told Jimmy I felt confident he would want it done now rather than later once the tables had pulled out from the walls.

The following morning, we had an elder meeting, which Jimmy presided over. He began the meeting with this statement: "Fellas, I think we have a problem with our project manager on our remodel of the youth building. He does not get what *wrap it up* means, so I think we should fire him." As he recommended this action, I thought to myself, *Hold on a minute. The problem isn't with the project manager. If there's a problem, then it's with me. I am the one who approved every single item of additional work.* So I raised my hand and said, "I don't think your problem is with the project manager. It is with me." One of the non-staff elders who was sitting next to me leaned over and whispered, "Tom, let's wrap it up." Again, my attitude leaked out, and I whispered back, "Oh, shut up!"

The conversation shifted from firing the project manager to discussing how they would deal with me. I remained calm on the outside, but I was angry and defensive on the inside. As they considered what to do with me, I was formulating a defense in my mind. *First,* I thought to myself, *overseeing this project wasn't on my written job description as the year began. Come to think of it, it still wasn't officially on it at all. Second, I only approved things I knew Jimmy would have approved if he knew all the circumstances and the project was under his oversight.* So what was the big deal? Based on my internal conversation, I had prepared my defense because now I was feeling abused and, therefore, justified in resisting what was decided about how I should be corrected.

After the meeting, I thought, *I am going to call a few of my elder friends this afternoon and plead my case.* But then my mind went to an even darker place. *No, wait. I think I'll just quit. If they think they can do a better job, then they can just have it!* As these thoughts stirred in my brain, the Lord intervened with a question: "Tom, are you going to let Me correct you?" In an instant, I shifted into "religious" mode and said, "Lord, is that You? It is your humble servant, Tommy. I am surrendered to You, and You can correct me any time." The Lord replied, "No, I can't! I have been trying to direct you, then correct you, but you will not listen. Right now, I am trying to teach you through this discipline, and you won't listen to that either." Then the Lord said something that really got my attention: "If you won't let me correct you in this one thing, then I won't be able to trust you with the plans I have for you in the future!"

God was telling me that if I was unsubmitted to the authority under which He placed me, and if I was unwilling to accept correction, then I had gone as far as I could in working for His Kingdom. Once I realized the implications of what the Lord was saying to me, I had an immediate attitude change. I confessed

I was wrong and that my response was rebellious and unsubmitted. I knew it and admitted what God knew and Jimmy (my boss) had felt. In my 22 years on staff at Trinity Fellowship, that was the only year I received a poor annual performance review. It was also the only year I did not get a full merit increase in my salary.

Submission to the authorities in this life reflects my submission to God's authority in heaven.

As I considered my thoughts and actions, I realized what I did wrong happened because of my hidden attitudes. If I had been submitted when I was told to "wrap it up," then I would not have approved even a single expense without first getting approval from Jimmy. Since I assumed and presumed approval even though I had been given a directive to "stop," I was showing myself to be both independent and rebellious. Jimmy was my best friend, but that did not mean I had the right to ignore his instructions based on what I thought he would approve without asking him first. Friendship, position, and trust cannot be played as trump cards to avoid accountability. Rather, accountability is your friend, and it will protect you.

Today, almost 40 years later, I still carry the lessons I learned from my mistake with the youth building. It reminds me that submission to the authorities in this life reflects my submission to God's authority in heaven. Responding with anger, disrespect, and pride toward authority mirrors the same attitudes we carry toward God. I realize I would very likely not be at Gateway Church today nor would I have experienced fruitful ministry for all these years if had I not learned this important lesson.

> Faithful are the wounds of a friend;
>   profuse are the kisses of an enemy.
>
> —Proverbs 27:6

Lesson 6

EVERY GENERATION HAS THE RESPONSIBILITY TO BUILD WEALTH.

Whatever you do, work heartily, as for the Lord and not for men, knowing that from the Lord you will receive the inheritance as your reward. You are serving the Lord Christ. For the wrongdoer will be paid back for the wrong he has done, and there is no partiality.

—Colossians 3:23–25, emphasis added

He also who had received the one talent came forward, saying, *"Master, I knew you to be a hard man, reaping where you did not sow, and gathering where you scattered no seed,* so I was afraid, and I went and hid your talent in the ground. Here you have what is yours." But his master answered him, "You wicked and slothful servant! You knew that I reap where I have not sown and gather where I scattered no seed? Then you ought to have invested my money with the bankers, and at my coming I should have received what was my own with interest."

—Matthew 25:24–27, emphasis added

Examine yourselves, to see whether you are in the faith. Test yourselves. Or do you not realize this about yourselves, that Jesus Christ is in you?—unless indeed you fail to meet the test! I hope you will find out that we have not failed the test.

—2 Corinthians 13:5–6, emphasis added

WHEN I WAS young, my dad taught me the importance of hard work and responsibility. As believers, we must live out our faith in each successive generation, which means it must reflect both hard work and the responsibility to steward our talents and opportunities. Every talent or opportunity carries with it a responsibility to make the most of it for God. Together, they open a way for us to walk by faith. As we follow the path that opens to us, our faith is a measurable expression of our trust in God for His promises and provision.

Our faith is a measurable expression of our trust in God for His promises and provision.

We can invest financial wealth, grow it, and pass its benefits down to our children and grandchildren. However, we can also squander it, take it for granted, and consume its life-giving benefits within a single generation. In a real sense, our faith operates in a similar way. It represents a living, current relationship with God that manifests in tangible expressions of trust through actions we take because we believe God's promises. Since faith is present and available in real time, it must be managed and grown in every generation. Each generation will experience the benefits of faith, but it must become active and grow in the present so it can live and thrive. Every day we take it for granted or ignore it only increases the risk that we will not pass it along to our descendants.

Have you heard the old axiom, "Shirtsleeve to shirtsleeve in three generations"? Financial planners often employ this adage, but it has more application than simply to the financial industry. This principle also applies to ministry and life in general. What is the point of this saying? It means that parents work hard to build wealth to pass along to the next generation, but over time that generation consumes, spends, and often wastes the wealth they received, leaving nothing or very little for their children (the third generation). Grandchildren often receive no inheritance left by the grandparents to their parents. The second generation's wasteful, uncontrolled desires consumed the resources left to them by their parents without thought for the third generation, which has to return to building wealth. This cycle repeats in many families.

Financial planners attempt to address this issue on behalf of the families they serve. They help those families who want to pass on their wealth multi-generationally to their children, grandchildren, and further generations by wisely protecting it from the wanton waste of a single consuming generation. They encourage the heirs to steward the original wealth and add to it, even while using it judiciously for their enjoyment and benefit.

James E. Hughes wrote about this issue in *Family Wealth— Keeping It in the Family: How Family Members and Their Advisers Preserve Human, Intellectual, and Financial Assets for Generations*. This book first captured my attention in the 1980s. Hughes served as an attorney and financial planner, and he asked himself, "How do the wealthiest families in the world keep and pass on their wealth multi-generationally?" How do they keep from falling prey to the financial planning axiom I mentioned at the beginning of this lesson? As I was reading his book, I realized that the principles Hughes discovered applied to more than just money. In fact, he discovered that those families who were able to overcome the axiom built a relational system that was focused on stewarding, building, and passing on their family wealth across multiple generations. In building this system of wealth management, they defined their wealth in more ways than just monetary terms. Money was only one of the components in these families' definition of "wealth." I found this concept fascinating, especially as it related to the spiritual blessings and relationship with God that I wanted to pass along to my children and grandchildren.

Scripture teaches that God is the source of all wealth. He is the one who gives us the power to gain wealth, and He does not attach sorrow with it. *Wealth, by its fullest definition, is the accumulation of five components: relationships, education, financial assets, stature of influence, and experience.* There is, however, *a sixth component of wealth* for those who love God and desire to reflect their love and service to Him. This component is the most important expression of our wealth. *It is the fruitful connection and relationship we have with God.* I am not referring to a religious association with Him; rather, I am talking about a personal relationship with the Lord Jesus Christ, which reflects an intimate connection with Him, followed by devoted service that comes from that connection. It is reflected in an ongoing desire and pattern to seek and serve Him.

In Psalm 103:2–5 David tells us to forget none of God's benefits and then lists what they are:

- forgiveness for all our iniquities
- healing for all our diseases
- redemption of our lives from destruction
- steadfast love and mercy
- satisfaction with good things
- renewed youth

As I read this Psalm again, I wondered, *Can those spiritual blessings be experienced and passed on multi-generationally?* You see, they are more than money, but if they could be purchased, their price would be so high that these blessings would be limited to only the wealthiest of people and their families. God has designed faithfulness to work in such a way that one of its expressions is wealth. It is a wealth that is more than money and can be passed on multi-generationally by being managed, increased, and enjoyed in each generation, ultimately leading to a stockpile of treasures in heaven.

God has designed faithfulness to work in such a way that one of its expressions is wealth.

It only makes spiritual sense that wealth is more than the accumulation of financial assets. From God's perspective, if wealth was solely reflected in the accumulation of financial assets, then it would mean that America and a few other countries who have the majority of the world's financial assets have been unfairly given wealth by God at the expense of the rest of the world. Does that mean that the others lost out in God's eyes? Is this really true? Of course, it isn't.

God is a good Father and does not withhold His blessings from some people while pouring them out on others. He has given all people and all families the same opportunity to receive what He has given to them, distributed it according to their abilities, and then tasked them with managing it well. If we properly steward God's blessings, then they will produce an increase in what we have, and we will qualify ourselves for Him to trust us with more. This principle is true for every type and category of wealth.

Also, we know that financial wealth doesn't, of its own accord, produce happiness or lead to a sense of purpose and destiny in our lives. People with great financial wealth are frequently unhappy, lonely, and isolated. God does not give wealth without connecting it to stewardship and purpose, because that would not reflect His loving nature. Jesus compared God's loving care as our Father to the loving care we give to our own children. He said, "If you then, being evil, know how to give good gifts to your children, how much more will your Father who is in Heaven give good things to those who ask Him!" (Matthew 7:11). God is never arbitrary with the ways He deals with His children. He is loving and wise and knows each of our abilities. He does not give any of us more than we can properly manage for His purpose and our benefit.

How does this concept relate to you and your children? Ask yourself these questions:

- *Am I following God's pattern as I bless my children with what I think are good gifts?*
- *How are the financial assets entrusted to me being stewarded by me and my children?*
- *Am I giving these wealth management principles consideration as I think about a wealth distribution plan for my family?*

When we understand and recognize that all we have belongs to God and that we are simply stewards or managers of what He has given to us, it transforms everything. It changes the way we spend, save, invest, view others, and offer ourselves in service to help others. It revolutionizes our purpose for living and working. With our focus on godly stewardship, we will understand God as a multi-generational God who desires for us to pass along to the next generation what we have built and accumulated in all six of the expressions of wealth that are ours to manage.

46

God expects us to increase the wealth that was passed on to us from our parents and grandparents. When we manage our wealth from this multi-generational, stewardship perspective, then we will stop consuming our wealth and begin building and investing it for God's Kingdom purposes. When we carry this perspective, we recognize our responsibility is to build the wealth that has been passed on to us. Only then do we experience a true accumulation of wealth. This perspective enables us to hand to the next generation resources that carry spiritual life and God's blessings rather than leaving things that come attached to pain and sorrow. The Bible clearly provides us this perspective when we look at the lives of Abraham, Isaac, and Jacob.

We are responsible to pass on to our children and grandchildren what God has entrusted to us. They are responsible to grow what they receive from us by managing and investing the resources, adding to that wealth, and then deploying it for God's Kingdom purposes in their own generations. They must also strive to develop the same perspective in their children. It is the perspective they received from us as their parents that their wealth is entrusted to them by God to be used for His purposes in their generation. The cycle repeats as they pass their accumulated wealth on to their children to be used in all its expressions for their joy and pleasure and for God's Kingdom purposes.

The next generation takes what it receives and builds on it, and the process continues multi-generationally. Through this process of generational faithfulness, each successive generation experiences more and more of the blessings and goodness of God in their own lives. Then they pass their experience on to their children and grandchildren.

Only when we see wealth as a resource entrusted to us both to maintain and to build will we be able to pass it on to the next generation. Once again, the most important expression of wealth we can have is our relationship with God. If we pass on the other five components of wealth but fail to guide our families into a relationship with God, then we fail to pass on wealth in its fullness. All true wealth starts with God as the foundation.

We must teach our children and grandchildren to love each other, to love the body of Christ, and to see themselves as ambassadors for God by serving people in their own generations. We should make it our goal to help them understand that every one of their attitudes and actions will affect how others view His Kingdom. This goal is true for every age and stage of their development. We are our children's most influential teachers and must keep this always on our mind. We can't successfully impart concepts if we don't live and reflect them in our own lives. At all times, we should be aware that our children will catch more from us through observation than they will from direct instruction. In that sense, both the wealthy and the poor play by the same rules in how they will prepare the next generation.

If you experience only one or two of the six components of wealth, then you will only pass along limited wealth to the next generation. In some ways, you will pass on just enough for your descendants to be dangerous. If you have not experienced any of these components, then you will have nothing to give them. If that is the case, then you are truly poor, and you bequeath the same poverty to your children.

Our children will catch more from us through observation than they will from direct instruction.

Each generation will either wholly consume what their parents and God have allowed them to have, or they will take what has been passed along and manage it with the wealth-building perspective of their parents. The total amount of the resources is not the primary concern; rather, it is the ability to steward and build that wealth that they must understand and apply to their life circumstances. That way they will overcome the "shirtsleeves to shirtsleeves" axion in their future generations. It is also true that if you have grown up in poverty and received no wealth, then you are not necessarily condemned to poverty. You can choose to be the first generation to build wealth. In any case, whether you have experienced wealth or poverty, you must choose for yours to become a diligent, wealth-building generation. Then your descendants will have to take on the responsibility to manage and build the wealth they have received from you.

How can you make sure yours is a wealth-building generation? First, you should add all six components to your family definition of wealth and allow them to influence your family investment portfolio. Perhaps your parents didn't receive an education, but you are pursuing one. Your parents may have had little influence on their work or community, but you have an opportunity for greater influence. Maybe your parents were working class, but you have become an entrepreneur and built your own successful business.

Second, you should add greater quantities of each of the six components of wealth to your family wealth portfolio through your efforts and your reliance on God.

HOW TO BUILD WEALTH

Once again, you must understand that the foundation for wealth building starts with the realization that all wealth belongs to God. This foundation is true even if you are Bill Gates, Warren Buffett, Jeff Bezos, or any of the other billionaires of the world. How, then, can you build wealth? The answer is simple yet profound.

1. RECOGNIZE YOU ARE A WEALTH BUILDER.

Since all wealth belongs to God, He distributes it as He sees fit, according to each person's abilities. No matter how much wealth you have received, God wants you to build on it. God's desire is for you to be a builder. Don't compare what He has given you to what another person has received. The act of comparison only leads to envy, jealousy, and dissatisfaction. It may even disincentivize you to the point that you ignore your own responsibility to be a good steward. Regardless of the amount of wealth God has allowed you to have, you can begin putting it to good use by investing and growing it.

Jesus laid out this principle in His parable of the talents (see Matthew 25). He told about an owner whose character represents God and had great wealth. This man called his three servants and distributed resources to each one according to their abilities. Two of the servants immediately took their portions of the resources and invested them, leading to an increase in wealth. The third, however, reacted out of fear, insecurity, laziness, and entitlement. This servant buried his resources in the ground to keep them safe and avoid risk until the owner returned. Jesus said that the master commended the first two servants but condemned the third because he was lazy and wicked.

It does not matter what God has given you. It makes no difference whether you are the first generation to build wealth or you come from a long line of wealth builders. The only thing that matters is for you to build wealth in your generation and work diligently to pass that wealth-building mindset on to the next generations, including your children and grandchildren.

2. LEARN ALL YOU CAN.

In every position or assignment, learn all you can and do your best. What you learn will transfer to your next assignment. Nothing is insignificant in God's plans and economy. As such, consider no assignment as either insignificant or beneath your dignity, because you are His servant and representative. Look to previous generations for examples to follow and don't let a sense of entitlement creep into your way of thinking.

Remember, if you had godly parents and grandparents, then they worked hard to pass along what you have received. They did not consider themselves entitled; rather, they knew that God had blessed them, so they took advantage of every opportunity given to them. They also did not consider any opportunities beneath them. They were willing to begin in a lower position because they saw it as a path to something greater. They applied themselves, learned, served, and ministered as they built wealth in their generation to pass on to their children.

I have heard some parents say they work hard so their kids will not have to do the same. While I appreciate their loving care for their children and grandchildren, this point of view creates entitlement in future generations rather than passing on a wealth-building mentality. Avoid every sense of entitlement as you work to achieve a healthy balance between dependence upon God's providence and your personal responsibility to act as a wealth builder.

3. REMEMBER YOUR PLACE OF EMPLOYMENT IS BOTH A BUSINESS AND A MINISTRY.

If you serve in vocational ministry for a church or another Christian ministry, you very likely see yourself as working for God. However, you might also work as a housekeeper, a teacher, a lawyer, or a doctor. In any case, you are God's child and thus a minister for Him. You are His servant first, regardless of your vocation. So no matter where you are employed or what your vocation is, you work for Him. Your first responsibility is to represent God and advance His Kingdom in people's lives.

Base your decisions on values that are anchored in God's Word, not just your own experiences or feelings. Every generation has unique challenges, which can cause a disconnection between the generations. For example, your choice in music probably won't be your children's selection. If you strongly oppose their musical tastes without considering the generational differences, then you will be fulfilling the "shirtsleeves to shirtsleeves" axiom through the resistance you express. Seek to understand their choices and scrutinize them only to make sure they reflect the values you hold as a family.

Your first responsibility is to represent God and advance His Kingdom in people's lives.

To keep the generational connection, make minimal and only necessary objections to the expressions of the younger generations and help them to recognize the values and cultural myths behind them. Make sure you explain your family's values and reinforce them to your children. Then help them understand why these are your values. Engage your children in conversations and ask them questions that will help them apply your family's values to the issues of their day.

Your family culture comes from your values, the people you hold high and admire, and your family's traditions. Your family culture will curate and steward the wealth that you worked so hard to produce. If you do nothing to pass along and protect your family culture, then you will, no doubt, squander the wealth that was passed along to you. You will enjoy its benefits yourself but leave little or nothing to pass along to your children and grandchildren. They will have to take up the task of building wealth from ground zero.

Adopting and exchanging unhealthy, ungodly values from new additions to your family will water down the godly values that have been previously established and passed down to you, your children, and your grandchildren. Ultimately, without a protected family culture, everyone will be left to do what seems right in their own eyes. That is the definition of anarchy.

4. UNDERSTAND WEALTH BUILDING AS A REFLECTION OF YOUR PARTNERSHIP WITH GOD.

Do not think of wealth as God's reward for your good efforts. Wealth does not reflect God's special pleasure or love for you as opposed to His displeasure with others. Don't concern yourself with how He allows wealth to be distributed. Also, recognize that wealth is not a zero-sum exchange. By that, I mean as you build your wealth, you are not reducing or eliminating someone else's. God's wealth is infinite just as He is infinite. He is not a socialist, feeling obligated to give to each of His children an equal amount. He gives to each according to their abilities and the expression of their stewardship. Therefore, we can rejoice with the successful wealth building of others while we are both challenged and inspired.

In the previously mentioned parable of the talents, the wicked servant who hid his wealth instead of building it had it taken away. That wealth was given to another servant who managed well. The wicked, lazy servant was no longer allowed to manage the owner's resources. Jesus said, "To everyone who has will more be given, and he will have an abundance. But from the one who has not, even what he has will be taken away" (Matthew 25:29).

Be a wealth builder in God's kingdom. Steward, nurture, and invest in the six components of wealth and join in partnership with Him to make the most of what He has given you. Then you will be able to hear Him say, "Well done, good and faithful servant, enter into the joy of your master!"

The blessing of the Lord makes rich,
and he adds no sorrow with it.

—Proverbs 10:22

Lesson 7

TAKE RESPONSIBILITY FOR YOUR MISTAKES.

Confess your sins to one another and pray for one another, that you may be healed. The prayer of a righteous person has great power as it is working.

—James 5:16

Therefore the redeemed of the Lord shall return, and come with singing unto Zion; and everlasting joy shall be upon their head: They shall obtain gladness and joy; and sorrow and mourning shall flee away.

—Isaiah 51:11 (KJV)

ARE YOU A leader? Are you working to expand your leadership influence? If so, it may seem that this lesson does not apply to you or is too elementary. However, it is both elemental and profound as it applies to your leadership. You may not think it speaks to your current position or even to what you hope to do in the future, but it really is essential to both your present and your future.

No leader or parent is perfect. No one is flawless in the role to which they've been assigned or aspire to fill. In fact, every single person is a work in progress. If you have been placed in a position of leadership, then never forget that God's hand put you there. And He can also remove you. How you lead is one more reflection of your stewardship before Him. Take note of this important fact: *everything rises and falls on leadership.* Decide today that how you lead will reflect God's presence and work in your life. Make humility, gratitude, and love your foundation as a leader who serves your Lord and Master.

TAKE RESPONSIBILITY FOR THE RESULTS

The first step toward leadership development is learning to *take responsibility for the results your team produces.* Recently, I listened to the audiobook version of *Extreme Ownership: How U.S. Navy Seals Lead and Win* by Jocko Willink and Leif Babin. These Navy Seal officers inspired and challenged me in my understanding of leadership principles. As I listened, I wanted to stand up straighter and do my best to be an authentic leader. With several real-life stories, they illustrated one of the greatest elements of the "Seal ethic": *leaders serve the people they lead.* This concept is also a biblical one. Leaders don't adopt a sense of entitlement and expect to be served. They set the example for others to follow. Leaders assume responsibility for their teams' mistakes and failures. If something happens under their leadership, even if they were not directly involved, then they take responsibility. They won't accept finger pointing or excuses. They only take ownership.

 **Leaders assume responsibility for their teams' mistakes and failures.**

This lesson has critical importance for anyone, but especially for aspiring leaders. If you mess up, then admit it. A true leader doesn't point to the circumstances or try to blame others. No, real leaders know that "the buck stops here." Navy Seals know that the factors influencing the outcome of their mission can change, so they construct plans with contingencies, which will ensure that their efforts produce success. Leaders anticipate, plan, and prepare for the unavoidable "what ifs."

A leader understands that leading a group comes with the responsibility for the outcome of the group's efforts. If the people under your leadership are unprepared for the unexpected, then it is not your team's fault—it is your fault as a leader. So don't make excuses. Instead, own the mistakes, flawed or inadequate planning, failed training, and shallow preparation. If someone under your oversight makes a mistake, then it is *your* responsibility because *you are the leader.* Take ownership of the mistakes. And take responsibility with your superiors and your team, because that is what genuine leaders do.

All of us want to be judged on our intentions rather than the actual results of our efforts. We plead our case by asking people to listen to our hearts and understand our motives. Then we want them to extend us grace for our failed actions or those of our team. I have observed this dynamic in every arena.

As a leader, husband, father, friend, overseer, and pastor, my heart is to do right. Have you ever had these thoughts: *Why can't people see my good intentions? Why won't they give me some credit even though my efforts didn't produce the intended outcomes? My heart really does want to do right and be right. Even worse, the people I depend on didn't carry their share of the load. How could they have failed to do their part when they knew what I expected? So we didn't get the results we expected. I mean, this really isn't my fault. It's theirs. They failed to execute the plan. Look at the effort I made, and I even took the team's intentions into consideration. We had a good plan, and I prepared them. I know we had the right strategy, but the outcome wasn't successful. So it must be their fault that we didn't produce the expected outcome.*

Here is the answer to that internal conversation: as a leader, you are responsible for both the execution and the results. At some point, you will fail to produce the expected results. Then what? You can't lay the blame for the results at someone else's feet. Your failure isn't because of your parents, your spouse, your children, or the poor performance of someone who works for you. No, the failed execution is your responsibility as a leader. Sure, people are flawed, and, like you, they make mistakes. But you will help no one by pointing fingers of blame. Focusing on someone else's failure is not a valid defense. Whining about their mistakes to your superiors will not ingratiate them to you. Avoid becoming punitive and dismissive toward others because you think they failed and made you look bad. Instead, start by asking yourself this question: *Why didn't my leadership on this project cause my team to make the right efforts to bring about the results we expected?*

In Willink and Babin's book, they share a story from their experience as Seal Team trainers. During training, every class member is placed on a seven-member team with other new recruits. In one exercise, each team is given a 200-pound rubber boat to carry. The senior recruit on each boat crew is made the leader. Then the teams are all put in extreme conditions. They are cold, tired, and sleep deprived. Meanwhile, a trainer is in their faces, barking commands and encouraging them to quit.

Under those severe conditions the teams compete in a race with one another. They must carry their boats down the beach and into the water. Next, they have to paddle the boat some distance into the water, go around a buoy, and then return to the beach. Winning teams are allowed a short rest while the losers continue racing other teams.

During these training exercises, Willink and Babin observed that one boat team (Boat Team 2) excelled over all the others and won most of the races. They also noticed that Boat Team 6 consistently lost by a margin of approximately 50 yards behind their opponents. Frustrated by losing, the members of Boat Team 6 could be heard shouting and screaming at each other, each blaming the other for the team's poor performance.

Based on the results of the initial races, the trainers agreed to conduct a leadership experiment with the recruiting class. They wanted to determine how much difference a leader makes in shaping a winning team. So they swapped the senior leaders from Boat Team 6 and Boat Team 2. In the first race after exchanging leaders, Boat Team 6 won, and they kept winning. The same recruits who had been losing by 50 yards were now defeating all the other teams. The only change made by the trainers was trading the team leaders.

This informal experiment proved a long-held Navy Seal axiom: *There are no bad teams—only bad leaders.* What had changed on these two teams? Only the leaders. A loser became a winner and vice versa. Admitting that your team's failure is due to your leadership rather than someone else's performance is a hard pill to swallow. Not every member of your team will be a star performer, but your responsibility is to lead every team member toward their best performance.

If you will take this one piece of advice, then it will help you as you grow in leadership: *don't defend yourself based on your intentions.* No one is going to call you a great leader because of your skill for justifying your mistakes. Instead, take responsibility for your actions. If you want to grow as a leader, then you must learn to take responsibility for the results you produce. Begin by evaluating the results you are producing in your own life. How are you leading yourself? Do your efforts produce the fruit you expect? Are you disappointed with the results in your personal life? Have you tried to blame others for your shortcomings? Ask yourself who you are holding accountable for the fruit in your life and start taking responsibility today.

LEARN FROM YOUR MISTAKES

Once you learn to take responsibility for your mistakes, regardless of who was involved or any other reason, then you are ready to move to this second step: *learn from your mistakes.* Life's tests are intended to teach you, and they will also produce endurance in you. New Testament writer James tells us this truth (see James 1:2–4). It is as though you are in a learning laboratory. Failure teaches you one way *not* to do something. Only insanity would lead you to follow the same path that already failed to produce. Learn and change but don't quit. Don't get down on yourself or beat yourself up verbally and emotionally. Identify what you need to change, do it, and then move on.

Learn this acronym: **F.I.D.O.** What does it mean? *Forget It and Drive On.* Put this in your mental bank and repeat it every time you or the people who work with you make a mistake. So you failed to produce the desired results? *Forget It and Drive On.* Learn from your mistakes, take responsibility, make the appropriate changes, and then **F.I.D.O.** If you will learn from your mistakes, then they won't disqualify you from future service. In fact, they actually qualify you because they are part of your learned experience. What will disqualify you is blaming others, getting down on yourself, or quitting out of discouragement. Don't disqualify yourself. **F.I.D.O.**

If you will learn from your mistakes, then they won't disqualify you from future service.

60

Be a leader and take responsibility. And as you do, don't accuse yourself or allow the enemy to do it. Apologize to the appropriate people and repent to God. Change your actions and **F.I.D.O.** Remember, God redeems and forgives you, so you must do the same for yourself and those you lead. The Bible says, "The eyes of the LORD run to and fro throughout the whole earth, to give strong support to those whose heart is blameless toward him" (2 Chronicles 16:9).

> If we say we have not sinned, we make him a liar, and his word is not in us.
>
> —1 John 1:10

Lesson 8

RESPECT AND HONOR THE PAST.

Do not move the ancient landmark that your fathers have set.

—Proverbs 22:28

"Honor your father and mother" (this is the first commandment with a promise), "that it may go well with you and that you may live long in the land."

—Ephesians 6:2

SECOND CHRONICLES 10 describes a generational transfer following the death of King Solomon. His son Rehoboam stood first in line to the throne of Israel. When Rehoboam was being installed as the new king, one of his father's advisors recommended that he not adopt his father's harsh policies. However, Rehoboam was a vain and foolish man who was blinded by his own pride. He refused to listen to wise counsel and instead responded, "My little finger is thicker than my father's thighs. And now, whereas my father laid on you a heavy yoke, I will add to your yoke. My father disciplined you with whips, but I will discipline you with scorpions" (2 Chronicles 10:10–11). Then Rehoboam followed through on his destructive promise, which ultimately caused the division of the unified county into the northern and southern kingdoms.

Like every person, you want to leave a mark within your own generation, and that is not wrong in itself. However, you make a grave mistake if you harshly judge previous generations rather than learning lessons from them. If simply throwing off the past is your major motivation, then you will inadvertently replicate the errors of previous generations instead of making the improvements you are seeking. This approach will steer you away from a path that God will bless.

In an effort to distinguish themselves from previous generations and to respond to the changes impacting their own, many emerging leaders are tempted to measure the shortcomings of past generations and point fingers at their flaws. As they highlight the failures of their parents and grandparents, they incorrectly interpret past policies and practices. They focus on how antiquated and out of touch the previous generation was for meeting the needs of the current one. They conclude that the ideas of the past are unworthy of being considered, adopted, or embraced. It is too easy to assume that meeting the needs of the current generation requires us to leave behind all the practices and values of the past so we can adopt "new" ways of thinking.

Breakthroughs in science and technology give us the ability to respond to our generation in ways that didn't exist or apply in the past. In a very short time, we have been introduced to innovations such as the internet, email, social media, video games, virtual reality, and artificial intelligence. Even so, I urge you to be cautious about changing the values of your parents, particularly those that are anchored in biblical principles. You may be facing pressures from the culture around you, but don't let them lead you astray. Decide you will work to learn how to apply those biblical principles to the new realities of your generation. Solomon wrote:

> What has been is what will be, and what has been done is what will be done, and *there is nothing new under the sun*. Is there a thing of which it is said, "See, this is new"? It has been already

in the ages before us. There is no remembrance of former things, nor will there be any remembrance of later things yet to be among those who come after (Ecclesiastes 1:9–11, emphasis added).

Solomon tells us that we are wise to consider his advice for addressing the issues presented in each new generation. Before you were born, your parents weren't as boring as you think they are now. Before you joined the organization where you now work, it wasn't as lethargic and bureaucratic as it appears to be now either.

Organizations and families have histories. Their histories are compilations of the events and circumstances that came together to influence them into becoming what they are today. Too often people and organizations are shaped by their pain rather than by balanced, healthy, and well–considered intentions and timeless values. Was it a reaction to pain or a healthy decision that formed your current organization? You won't know unless you make the effort to explore what lies beneath the surface. Try your best to understand the history behind the organization you are now tempted to criticize.

Learn the reason why things are the way they are before you criticize them or attempt to change them. Your parents and some of those leading the organization you are criticizing were impacted, and in some cases hurt, by circumstances that influenced their actions. Their unhealed pain could be the source of the behavior you are criticizing. You can identify the deformation of your organization or your family and criticize its impact on you, feeling certain that you would do nothing like what had been done. Maybe that would be true, but you won't know if you don't discover what they were responding to in the first place.

Your parents may have ignored important issues in their own generation, which leaves you to deal with the dysfunction in your generation. You will either respond to it, or you will pass it on to the following generations. Remember, it is too easy to judge the past from today's perspectives and insights. I caution you not to form a response before you understand the causes of those wounds of the past.

It is too easy to judge the past from today's perspectives and insights.

Seek understanding before you move on to action. Avoid judgments of the past if you don't fully understand the real causes. Before you were born, your family was experiencing life. Before you were employed by your current organization, many things transpired. Some of the things that happened in the past were great. Those great things are what we proudly showcase for others to see and know. However, other events were dark and embarrassing. These things form a hurtful history, which most of us are reticent to discuss. The path of least resistance is to ignore the ugliness of our families or our organizations. Most of us would rather bury embarrassing events in the past than face them head on. So we choose to hide them and leave them for future generations to discover. They will have to face the results without knowing the causes because we have joined previous generations in one grand coverup.

There are reasons why your family or your organization developed their cultures and policies. Perhaps they needed to take certain actions so they could meet particular needs and grow. They may have been reacting to tragic and devastating events. Their cultures may have roots in a simple desire to protect the family or the organization from danger or hurt. Regardless of the reasons, motivations, or impact, they most likely wanted to help and protect people. Try your best to understand before you criticize and then be cautious and wise about changing things until you know why they were put in place. This is how you show respect for the past.

Could it be that your organization grew so big and cumbersome because they developed great systems that caused them to succeed? Those systems were born out of need, experience, and pain. Identify and respect those systems. Why were they put in place? Answer that question before you begin changing them. Understand and embrace the systems before you blow them up.

If you want to remain relevant and meet the needs of your generation, then some of the systems of the past may indeed need to change. Organizations that refuse to change over time will become irrelevant, obsolete, and relics of the past that will only be discussed in colleges, business schools, and family therapy sessions. They will serve as examples of "what not to do." Don't hold on to the past with a fearful grip that things might change. You don't know what the final outcome will be, but you can't remain frozen, stuck, and unable to respond.

My dad was a man of his word. In his generation, a man's word sealed with a handshake formed a binding contract. In my generation, though, many people thought that keeping your word simply on a handshake was unrealistic and did not allow flexibility for changing circumstances. They changed the way they thought about the importance of a person's word and commitment. Before long, that way of thinking fostered other questions, such as these: "Is there really absolute right or wrong that can apply to every circumstance? Doesn't the situation determine if something is right or wrong? When you give your word in one set of circumstances, does that mean it's binding in all circumstances, even if the conditions change?"

My generation began focusing on the need for judgment and "decisionism" that allowed for nimble responses to changing circumstances. Every circumstance called for a decision, and everything was a dilemma. Even Christians started thinking about moral questions in this way. Christians in previous generations didn't focus so much on the impact of changing circumstances on their decisions because they knew God had *already decided* how people should believe and behave. Christians told the truth because Christians are *by definition* truth-tellers. A new way of thinking about moral issues started permeating every aspect of life, and it was taught extensively in our schools. We learned that there is no truth with a capital "T." All ethical questions are quandaries that no one can really solve, so everyone can do what is right in their own individual eyes. The strict adherence to truth, morality, character, and commitment by my father's generation gave way to a whole new moral world in mine—a world of "situation ethics." Even worse, no one could say how Christians should behave, because there was no longer even agreement on what defined a "Christian."

My dad recognized this moral shift was happening, and he knew situation ethics was based on some faulty assumptions. He told me to keep my word, regardless of the situation. My generation might have been trying to change the definition of morality, but in the Lane family, Christians are still truth-tellers who keep their word. Period. One summer, as a young boy with a lot of energy, I asked my dad if I could use the family lawnmower to start my own lawnmowing business. He gave me his blessing, and I began canvassing the neighborhood for lawnmowing customers. Finally, I got my first customer. She was a widow who lived only a few blocks over from our house. She told me she was having guests on the weekend and needed her lawn done by Friday. I thanked her for the business and agreed to have it done in time for her guests.

But by the time Friday rolled around, my eagerness had waned. Lawnmowing just didn't seem that important anymore. My buddies invited me to play baseball on the field by the school, so I blew off my lawnmowing commitment. At the time, it seemed like the right choice. It certainly felt more important to be with my friends than to keep my word to my new lawnmowing customer. That is, until later that day.

My family was eating dinner that evening when the phone rang. I'm sure you can guess who was calling. I could only hear my mother's end of the conversation: "Oh, he did? He what? Well, let me let you talk with Jim." That's when my dad took the phone. And I could only hear his end of the conversation as well: "Oh he did? Yes, he will. Right now. We are on our way over." He handed the phone back to my mother, and then he turned to me and asked, "Did you say you would mow a lawn by today?"

That's when I got a sudden case of amnesia. At first, I acted like I had no recollection of committing to do a lawn. Then the truth came out. I confessed that I had made that commitment, but my friends wanted me to play baseball instead. My dad replied, "Get up right now. We are going to go mow a lawn." I offered a weak objection: "Right now? But we are eating." He responded, "We will keep our word and then eat after that." He marched me over to that widow's house. Then he stood and watched as I mowed every inch of her lawn, making sure it was perfect. Then he told me to edge it, rake up the clippings, bag them, and sweep the driveway and sidewalks.

When I finally finished the job, my dad turned to the lady and said, "There you are, and this one is on us." All that work and no pay?! That really hurt. But I didn't dare say a word. My dad was teaching me a lesson. If I had mentally counted that money for my piggy bank, he was teaching me that I had already spent it by compromising my integrity and the reputation of my family. It was a lesson about the importance and priority of keeping my word, and that value still applied in my generation. Feelings and circumstances may change, but our values should transcend situational variables.

How should you respect and honor the past? You do it by learning the values of your parents' and grandparents' generations and then contextualizing them to the contemporary situations and circumstances of the current generation. Methods fluctuate from one generation to the next, but values don't. If values need to be adjusted because of a better grasp on the truth and God's will, then those changes should come slowly and be based on good intentions, careful consideration, and wise application with help from those in authority over you.

When a well-defined value system is handed down from your parents and grandparents, then you have an excellent place to start. Define and articulate those unchanging values. The writer of Hebrews tells us that Jesus is the same today, yesterday, and forever (Hebrews 13:8). God does not change.

> God is not man, that he should lie,
>   or a son of man, that he should change his mind.
> Has he said, and will he not do it?
>   Or has he spoken, and will he not fulfill it? (Numbers 23:19).

Values rooted in the Bible do not change. Discover those biblical values and live by them as you apply them to every circumstance. Don't spend your efforts trying to develop your own values; instead, make every effort to learn God's values.

Values rooted in the Bible do not change.

If you did not have godly parents who passed on godly values, then I will give you a good biblical place to start. Keep your word and be a truth-teller. Treat others as you would want them to treat you. Love people purely and passionately, as much as you love yourself. Honor God with your life. Don't take what isn't yours. Don't allow immorality to have any place in your life. Respect life and work to protect it. Don't kill people with actions, thoughts, or words. Take these biblical values and make them your own, Apply them to your life's circumstances and situations. Then pass them on to your children and grand-children. You show respect and honor for the past when you live by these values. And you make God your partner as you minister in the world.

Remember your leaders, those who spoke to you the word of God. Consider the outcome of their way of life, and imitate their faith. Jesus Christ is the same yesterday and today and forever.

—Hebrews 13:7–8

Lesson 9

EXCELLENCE IS A REFLECTION OF EFFORT AND ATTITUDE.

You are the salt of the earth, but if salt has lost its taste, how shall its saltiness be restored? It is no longer good for anything except to be thrown out and trampled under people's feet. You are the light of the world. A city set on a hill cannot be hidden. Nor do people light a lamp and put it under a basket, but on a stand, and it gives light to all in the house. In the same way, *let your light shine before others, so that they may see your good works and give glory to your Father who is in heaven.*

—Matthew 5:13–16, emphasis added

The earth brought forth vegetation, plants yielding seed according to their own kinds, and trees bearing fruit in which is their seed, each according to its kind. And God saw that it was good.

—Genesis 1:12

I AM ATTRACTED to excellence. I love to drive down a street and see a well-kept home, neat and clean with a well-manicured lawn. Whether it is a new construction or 50 years old, I appreciate the care the owners give to their property. In fact, well-maintained older homes with immaculate yards have a beauty and attraction all their own.

I also love to see a clean car of any age or style, waxed and glistening in the sun. I enjoy hearing a well-crafted presentation delivered with confidence as the fruit of diligent preparation. I love to see an organization that operates with efficiency, empowers its people, has a clearly-defined mission, and displays its values through every action.

I believe that deep within each of us is a yearning for excellence. When we see it reflected in something, our hearts cry out, *Yes!* It grabs our attention like a tractor beam with gravitational pull. The reason excellence draws us is because God built within us an attraction to it. Excellence captures our attention because God is excellent in all that He is and does. At our core, we want to reflect Him. When people recognize they are living outside of excellence, they know something is missing, even if they can't name it. It is because they are really living outside of what God wants for their lives.

Excellence captures our attention because God is excellent in all that He is and does.

Excellence is not a natural result of having money. It does not come from the newest and most expensive things someone might display to elicit the envy of others. The devil has a counterfeit for excellence, and it is made up of these worldly displays of wealth and power. Real excellence begins with an attitude that leads us to give our best with what we have regardless of the size of the platform on which we stand or the class of people in the crowd. Excellence has nothing to do with money but everything to do with effort, attitude, and stewardship reflected in our service to God. Excellence is the expression of our best effort crafted from the time and resources available to us. Excellence is not associated with perfection. Perfection is based on results, whereas excellence reflects the underlying effort and attitude that bring about the results.

Excellence corresponds to influence like wattage relates to a lightbulb. If you want to have great influence, then be excellent in all your efforts. God calls us to excellence, and He simply will not allow us to move on to a greater platform or gain greater influence if we neglect excellence. He assigns us to be stewards of our talents, abilities, and resources, and He wants us to use them to produce and display excellence. God is committed to our success, and it pleases Him when we give our best efforts using the resources available to us.

If you measure the success of your results by perfection, you may find it surprising or even shocking that God will say to those who pursue excellence yet have lesser results: "Well done, good and faithful servant! Enter into My rest." However, if you focus on excellence as a reflection of your service to God, then you have God as your partner, and you will find that He will take your faith and diligence on His behalf and count it as "good."

Excellence is a quality you will develop in the everyday and mundane parts of your life, when no one but God is looking. Your progress toward excellence is revealed in this test: how do you respond to the opportunities that open to you? Are you fixated on performance and focused on perfection as the outcome? You will be shocked when you find out that what God is really looking for is excellence rather than perfection, and the two are not the same in their expression. Have you assumed you failed if your results weren't perfect? You may have even condemned yourself. Did you know that your results can be perfect, but they may still not be excellent? If you measure yourself by the standard of perfection, then the slightest mistake will ruin the outcome. Or you may lower your standards so that you can celebrate even a mediocre effort. If you plan mediocre results, then you will not give your best effort. You'll only do enough to meet your lower expectations.

Are you being tested in some area of your life right now? Is this test stretching your ability to bring about a "perfect" result? Do you worry that someone or some group will reject you if your performance isn't perfect? If all of this is true, then you need to embrace the reality that their expectation isn't what God is asking of you. He is looking for excellence rather than perfection. He also allows open book tests—you just have to open the book! Ask, seek, and knock as you search the Bible and discover the principles and character qualities that will help you give your best effort. Understand that God will allow you as many efforts as you need to apply the things you are learning to produce excellence through your best effort.

Unlike some recent changes in the US educational system, God won't give you a passing grade just to make you feel better or to move you on to the next level to make room for someone else coming behind you. He wants you to learn the lessons of excellence for you to pass the test. You may have heard your parents, your pastor, your teacher, or your coach say, "If it is worth doing, it is worth doing right the first time." So give your best effort the first time and every time.

You also may have heard that with God, the journey is the destination. That thought may be challenging to you, especially if you are a "get it done" type of person. God is more interested in *how* you are producing the result than He is about the actual result. God is in the business of providence and miracles, so He can take your efforts and fix them, multiply them, or even nullify them. The Bible contains many stories where He does exactly one of those acts. God is more interested in quality and thoroughness than He is in the speed with which you accomplish a task.

 **God is more interested in quality and thoroughness than He is in the speed with which you accomplish a task.**

I can imagine that if you are a fly-by-the-seat-of-your-pants type of person, then this lesson may be causing you heartburn. Nevertheless, I need to break the news to you. Excellence can't be produced by taking a laissez-faire approach. It requires diligence, faithfulness, and consistent effort. King Solomon taught this principle:

> Whoever is slothful will not roast his game,
>   but the diligent man will get precious wealth
>   (Proverbs 12:27).

Consider the reality of that statement. In a day when people couldn't go to a local grocery store to buy food, they would ask themselves, "What am I hungry for today?" Once they decided what they wanted to eat, they then had to determine the best method to kill it. Would it be by bow and arrow? Would they have to trap it? Or would it be by some other method?

Once someone decided on the method to get the animal, it could take all day to track it, capture it, and kill it. By then, the person was ravenous. Rather than field dressing the kill to take it back to their tents to cook it, hungry hunters would rip strips of raw meat from the carcass to eat so they could satisfy their hunger. Solomon says lazy men are like this proverb. They take shortcuts and find the quickest way possible to produce results.

If a hunter doesn't plan and prepare for the hunt, he may or may not be successful and could end up living from day to day. In an effort simply to survive, he will skip steps to get to the desired result—food. Solomon calls a man who eliminates necessary steps to reach a conclusion "slothful" or lazy. Short-cut thinking will produce quicker results, but it may also introduce weaknesses and mistakes, which could prove deadly. If meat isn't cooked, then it can cause disease or even death. Solomon declares that a diligent commitment to hunt, kill, field dress, cook, and then eat without cutting steps is a precious possession and reflects an excellent effort.

Have you been tempted to take shortcuts so you can arrive at a quick and easy result? If we are really honest, almost all of us have given in to the temptation to cut out steps at some point to reach the desired results. Has this way of operating become your lifestyle? If it has, then beware—you are on a lazy path that will never lead you to excellence. Even worse, it may take you toward devastating consequences in the very near future.

Producing excellence requires a steady pace and effort. It takes time, and you can't produce it through impatience. Do you monitor the pace your life takes? Do you manage your schedule so you won't be overcommitted? Or are you running from one appointment to the next with very little preparation? If you want to project excellence, then you must govern your commitments and the pace of your activities.

Do you know how to say "no"? Until you learn to say it, you will miss great opportunities while you take on responsibilities that are less important and cause you to be overcommitted in your schedule. Saying "no" means you will need a process for evaluating what is most important so you can protect yourself and your time. Start today by embracing a "less is more" philosophy and carefully evaluate the opportunities that come your way. Don't buy into the idea that God is in every opportunity that comes before you. If you think that way, then you will assume every opportunity is God-ordained, and that simply is not true. You are not missing out or disobeying God if you manage what you can do with a focus on excellence and limit what only you can do to guard against producing mediocre results. Once you take stewardship of your time and resources seriously, you'll no longer run yourself ragged to the point of burnout.

If you are the kind of person who has difficulty limiting your activities, then you very well may be walking a path of mediocrity rather than excellence. Focus your efforts on doing less, and you will create the time and space necessary to produce excellent results. Your light will shine brighter if you become known for your excellence rather than your packed schedule.

Jesus tells us to let our lights shine (see Matthew 5:16). Let excellence shine from your life so people will be drawn to you, and thus they will be attracted to God. Excellence will reflect His nature and character in your life and will encourage others to follow your example.

Whoever is slothful will not roast his game,
but the diligent man will get precious wealth.
—Proverbs 12:27

Lesson 10

LIVE YOUR LIFE IN
A GODLY RHYTHM.

You shall remember that you were a slave in the land of
Egypt, and the Lord your God brought you out from there
with a mighty hand and an outstretched arm. Therefore the
Lord your God commanded you to keep the Sabbath day.

—Deuteronomy 5:15

Come to me, all who labor and are heavy laden, and I will give
you rest. Take my yoke upon you, and learn from me, for I am
gentle and lowly in heart, and you will find rest for your souls.
For my yoke is easy, and my burden is light.

—Matthew 11:28–30

ARE YOU A person who is typically late, early, or mostly on time?
The answer to that question depends on how you manage your
time and the pace you allow your life to take. I'm sure you've
heard there are 1,440 minutes in a day. Regardless of whether
you are rich or poor, you have exactly the same number of
minutes each day as every other person in the world. However,
some people get more from their minutes than others. I admit
that I never even thought about how many minutes or seconds
I had in a day until I reached my early thirties. I also never
thought about living my life in a rhythm. Instead, I would

default to filling my day as full as I possibly could without ever saying "no" to anyone or declining any opportunity.

As you can imagine, I was routinely late for appointments. It's not that I wanted to be late, but I was, and it was terribly frustrating for my wife and children. I wasn't on time to commitments I made. My norm was about 10 to 30 minutes behind schedule. Every time I dragged in late, I would feel bad and apologize profusely. But I still kept being late. That is, until one day I had an encounter with my best friend and pastor, Jimmy Evans.

My office was immediately across the hall from Jimmy's. When our doors were open, I could hear his conversations. One day, I overheard his assistant ask if he could meet with a couple for counseling that afternoon. He shocked me with his response. He told her there was no way he could see them that day but to offer them an appointment later in the week. After his assistant left his office, I stepped across the hall and asked Jimmy why he lied. He responded, "What do you mean?" I said, "I heard your conversation, and I know you don't have anything on your schedule this afternoon. But you said there was no way you could meet with that couple because you were too busy?"

Jimmy took a quiet pause to consider how he would reply to me. Then he said, "How can you know so much about budgeting your finances and so little about managing your time?" At first, I thought he was evading my question, so I asked, "What does that have to do with your calendar this afternoon?"

Jimmy's response expanded my understanding and started a change in me. He said, "Time is like money. It has to be managed and budgeted to make sure there is enough to spend on your priorities." I had never heard that, nor had I thought about time in that way before. Jimmy continued, "Tom, just like your budget focuses and prioritizes the amount you spend and where you spend your money, you also need a budget for

your time. That way you will know where and how to invest it."
I had heard the saying, "You're wasting time," but I had never
thought about it the way Jimmy did.

**Time is like money. It has
to be managed and budgeted to
make sure there is enough
to spend on your priorities.**

He told me he had to do some study for speaking and had
reserved the afternoon for that purpose. If he gave up his
preparation time to counsel the couple, he would be doing
the budgeting equivalent of "robbing Peter to pay Paul." He
would be giving his time to the couple and robbing from his
preparation time for an upcoming speaking engagement. It
would have either left him unprepared or required him to
take time from his family or other priorities to prepare for
his speaking schedule. That is why he said, "No." He truly was
busy, even though it wasn't with the people who were booked
on his calendar.

Until that day, the way I managed my time was the way
some people manage their budgets. If I had an open slot in my
schedule, then it was like having money in my checking account,
which meant I could spend it. I often spent time I didn't have
at the expense of other commitments I had previously made.
That is why I was regularly late and had a terrible "time reputation" with my family and friends.

Has anyone ever trained you on time management? Were you
taught how to develop a rhythm for your life, or were you left to
learn it on your own? My parents were on-time people. I think
they tried to teach me how to be an on-time person, but somehow

I did not get the concept of pace, rhythm, and time management. I lived my life and my commitments at full throttle.

As we are growing up, we are introduced to and instructed about rhythm, pace, and commitments from our parents as part of our development. Our instruction occurs either by intentional effort or by example. If your parents didn't understand the process of rhythm and pace for their lives but were overcommitted and stressed out, then how could they show you the way? Children in these situations are left untrained and are therefore forced to learn it on their own (or suffer the consequences of lateness, stress, and burnout).

We need to learn the rhythms of work, home responsibilities, recreation, worship, and rest. I believe God intended for us to learn from our parents' instructions and examples. They may have done their best to train us, but like so many things in our lives, we either embrace what we have been taught or react to it by forming judgments and making inner-vows. Then we live in reaction to what we have judged and vowed.

No matter how we developed our concepts of pace, rhythm, and time management, the way we manage these aspects of our lives has a dramatic effect on our success and influence. Without proper training at home, we will need to add that sometimes uncomfortable instruction from influential sources such as bosses, spouses, mentors, and friends to fill in the developmental gap. These people will need to help us identify what we should be doing or not doing, along with how frequently we should be doing it. They will help us identify the number of commitments we should reasonably make for a healthy life.

In addition to the people I just mentioned, there is another source of instruction and help. The Holy Spirit will guide and convict us when our lives begin to get off course. We need the

Holy Spirit's perspective on our pace and balance, which should be reflected in the commitments we both make and keep.

As believers, our behavioral road map is God's Word. Scripture is very intentional when it addresses the rhythm of our lives. We are encouraged to work, rest, fellowship, and meditate in a systematic way. God encourages us to guard ourselves against the extremes of laziness and workaholism.

Life isn't divided into semesters; rather, it is lived and measured in days, weeks, months, and years. These time blocks can then be grouped into seasons. In real life you don't get summers off, and you don't fully complete your work only to begin again a few months later. Few, if any, employers will ever be interested in helping you "find" yourself. God is the one who is most interested in your rhythm and pace. He wants you to find yourself in Him. He is committed to helping you fulfill your purpose and destiny, and He stands ready to assist if you will only ask Him. He cares about your physical, emotional, and spiritual health and wants you to pace yourself so that you can accomplish what matters most in your life.

There is a considerable focus in today's world on the health of our bodies, souls, and spirits. But we are still stressed out, sleepless, and saddled with greater work and life demands than any previous generation. We are killing ourselves, and for what? More money? More prestige? A better reputation? More fun? We don't know how to dedicate ourselves to a lifegiving rhythm or a sustainable pace.

We have lost many of the values of the past, such as showing our reverence for God by honoring the Sabbath and taking one day to recreate ourselves physically, emotionally, and spiritually. At the present, people feel guilty if they cease from their work, enjoy their families, or pause to give God His rightful place in their lives. At one time, the expectation of society was to keep the Sabbath, but today there is equal pressure *not* to keep it.

As followers of Jesus, we need to build into our schedules a rhythm that will allow for emotional and spiritual recovery after we have extended ourselves in care and service to others. Of course, we should live outside ourselves by investing in and helping others, but that effort will take a spiritual and emotional toll on us, sometimes equal to the exhaustion we feel from strenuous labor. This realization underscores the importance of learning how to slow down and rest. All types of work, including those that are physical, mental, emotional, and spiritual, require recovery time for us to give our best effort.

You may not know how to incorporate rest into your already busy life. However, don't let that be your top concern. God will lead you to the pace and rhythm He knows you need. Don't be worried that you will displease Him or miss your opportunity for promotion or advancement if you focus on the pace that is sustainable for healthy living. If you pause to honor God with a day of rest and focus on renewing yourself, then you will actually please Him in your obedience, and He will partner with you by leading you to quiet waters and places of rest. Living in the center of God's will sometimes requires patient waiting. And waiting on God requires you to know and live in His rhythm rather than according to an anxious pace.

Living in the center of God's will sometimes requires patient waiting.

I want the thoughts I am sharing with you in this lesson to start you on the path of finding rhythm, pace, and rest. You will spend the rest of your life broadening your understanding and figuring out how to apply what you learn. No matter where you are on your journey of discovery, I encourage you to walk further down the path of God's rest. If you have been side-tracked by busyness, distraction, or overcommitment, then I hope to help you get back on track. You will need to learn how to exercise your faith and obediently follow God's leading so you can experience and reflect the benefits of rhythm, pace, and rest.

A few years ago, I was thinking about how I understood Sabbath rest while I was growing up. I knew God had commanded His people to "honor the Sabbath day to keep it holy" (see Exodus 20:8–11). The church my family attended taught me that Sunday was the Sabbath and honoring God meant I should go to church, take an afternoon nap, deny myself things that I enjoyed, and put my focus on God. That may not have been the total content of their teaching, but that was how I interpreted and applied it. It was not very enjoyable, to be honest.

Was that your model too? Or have you simply fallen in line with a culture that encourages you to work hard, play hard, and repeat? Without a correct model of Sabbath, it is no wonder that our society doesn't know how to find rhythm, pace, and rest. Many people work 60–80 hours every week and then run to the lake, the mountains, or their children's sporting events on the weekend. The activity changes, but they are just as busy as they were all week long. Their busy weekend does not renew them.

Around the time that I was reflecting on God's rhythm and pace for our lives, I met with a friend at Starbucks. The purpose of the meeting was pastoral, and he initiated it. He wanted to talk about some things on his heart but not specifically about Sabbath rest. I arrived a little early and opened my laptop to access the store's Wi-Fi network. I intended to do some work while I waited from my friend to arrive. The web sign-on procedure took my browser immediately to the Starbucks home page. The lead article was a TED Talk by Stefan Sagemeister, a graphic designer, and was entitled "The Power of Time Off." It was about the importance of taking a sabbatical.

I am always amazed at the way God provides us with timely enlightenment. I was also impressed that Starbucks was sharing this content. Stefan was upfront with the admission that he is not a religious man. Nevertheless, he testified that his design business required his team members to renew their creativity by taking time off every seven years so they could be renewed and refreshed. Otherwise, their creativity became dull, and they merely rehashed old ideas on new projects. In response to his observations, Stefan decided to close his New York City design studio every seven years to take a one-year sabbatical. The purpose was for his employees to rest, refresh themselves, and recreate their passions, creativity, and energy. He outlined his journey toward discovery, renewal, and the implementation of what he experienced during his sabbatical year with its impact on his business.

As I listened, I thought the idea sounded great but also seemed unrealistic. What business or church could do what he did and close down operations for a year by simply putting a sign on the door with the following notice: "We are out on sabbatical and will return in a year"? Unlike his company, the church would go out of business, or at the very least, remain small, generate little impact, and cause us to live in a constant state of "launch," never really growing to maturity. At least that was my reaction as I listened to his talk.

Then a thought came to me. There are 52 weeks in a year and seven years in a biblical sabbatical cycle. Seven years times 52 weeks equals a total of 364 weeks. My mind quickly did the math, and I thought, *Wow! God knew we would not take a year away from our businesses, so He built a rest cycle into the rhythm of the life He wants us to lead.* If we will take one day out of every seven to rest and renew, then at the end of seven years, we will have rested 364 days. We will have taken one year off. If we practice a Sabbath day every week, we are taking a year off in bite-size increments every seven years. God has made it that easy, yet we fail to follow His command consistently and live in the rest He intended. We work at a frantic pace and fill every second with some activity. We live worn out, burned out, and without the creative energy we need to work well.

As I learn to live in God's rhythm and pace (and by the way, I am still learning), I experience rest and renewal as God intended. I am passionate, creative, engaged, and fun most of the time. I recognize that fatigue and stress increase when the rhythm and pace of my life are out of alignment with God's plan. And in the moments when I fail to recognize it, my wife helps me see the impact of overwork on me and our family.

The purpose of Sabbath is to connect us with God. As we connect with Him, it will be on a level that touches, excites, and renews our senses in a variety of expressions. We reconnect and realign with our God-given purposes. These new engagements with Sabbath won't be like the boring ones I experienced when I was young.

The purpose of Sabbath is to connect us with God.

HOW DO YOU VIEW YOUR WORK?

How can you invest your life and make sure you align yourself with God's purposes? Here are three possible ways to view your work:

1. YOUR JOB

You job is what you do for money. You may work from 8 am to 5 pm or follow different hours, but all the while you are looking forward to the weekend. Then you pour yourself into your hobby or other leisure activities, searching for a path to leveling and renewal. Still, you don't find a place of deep rest.

2. YOUR CAREER

Your career is the broader expression of the collective efforts of your life over a span of time. It is somewhat more connected to your "calling" than just a job, so you are more engaged and focused on improving your knowledge and skills. You make sacrifices to pour your time, energy, and efforts into building the collective results you desire. You want advancement and promotion, yet you wonder if the reward is worth the cost as you see the toll your career is taking on your health and family. You know your life is out of balance, but you're not sure what to do.

3. YOUR CALLING

Your calling is directly connected to your purpose, so it is intrinsically fulfilling. It reflects your passions and is so satisfying that you would do it even if you weren't paid, as long as you could still afford to meet your basic needs. When you find your calling, then rhythm, pace, and rest are naturally a part of your life because you are living it as God intended. You willingly answer Jesus' invitation to come to Him when you are weary and heavy laden, because you know He will give you rest (see Matthew 11:28). In Him there is no debilitating worry, anxiety, or stress. God's calling is not an all-out schedule, which will burn up the oil of God's presence in your life, nor will it consume your health or your family.

When you follow your calling and live in the rhythm and pace God intended, He will give you these four-fold benefits:

- Your job will become a reflection of your calling, and it will align you with your purpose.
- Your life will become enjoyable and manageable again as you live at a sustainable pace.
- God's blessings will be released to you in the form of creativity and revelation, which will spawn innovation.
- Your work will become more impactful as it is influenced by rest, creativity, and energy, which will be renewed and refreshed because of the pace and rhythm you have implemented in your life.

Does this sound attractive to you? What is the process for you to manage the rhythm and pace of your life? How can you incorporate a godly rhythm? It begins with the recognition that you must manage your time and commitments. You must be willing to admit that the default pace of your life with the pressures and demands from multiple sources is out of control. You have to become desperate enough to want to change. The routine of your work and the activities related to your family, friends, and hobbies consume energy and naturally push you toward overinvolvement and burnout. These things draw on the physical, emotional, and spiritual energy of your life, so you must be renewed through rest rather than by simply changing your activities.

When the energy demands of your life exceed the capacity of your reserves, you will experience your own "brown outs," like those of an overstressed electrical grid. Even worse, these demands can lead to a complete outage—a total depletion of the necessary energy to power all your activities. You must become an energy manager and evaluate your calendar and the schedule it reflects. Measure the demands on your mental, physical, emotional, and spiritual energy grid. When you are experiencing "peak" demand, you need to have the power to supply the energy required. You need to follow the peak times with days of lower activity and slower pace that will allow for rest and renewal.

When your work calls on you to use skills that are not among your strongest ones, then you must acknowledge that the energy demands will be greater. You will have to adjust the demands of other areas of your life, including hobbies, extracurricular activities, social commitments, and vacations. If you take vacations that are high in activity and intensity, then you will need to build in some days for rest and renewal either during or after your vacation. If you don't build in some rest days, then you will return worn out rather than renewed. You will need some time when you return to work so you can recover from your vacation. Have you ever returned from a vacation actually more exhausted than before you left? And if you never take time out of your work for a vacation, then you need to reevaluate balance in your life.

MAKING THE MOST OF SABBATH

Once you start viewing your schedule as an "energy grid," you will be ready to address your need for Sabbath. God gave Sabbath as a command, not as a suggestion. In both Deuteronomy 5 and Exodus 20, God traces the roots for Sabbath back to His design and care for our lives. We can completely ignore this command, but we do so at our own peril. To make the most of Sabbath in your life, incorporate these four things:

1. RENEW

Unplug from your daily responsibilities and use your resources, including finances, talents, relationships, interests, and technology, to re-approach life. Don't give up the things you enjoy; rather, limit the demands that drain your emotional and spiritual energy.

2. REVIEW

Take stock of your interests, particularly those things you have wanted to do but have put off because you haven't had the time, energy, or resources to accomplish them. If they are valid interests, can you look at them in a new way and perhaps even accomplish them? Ask yourself, *What am I doing that someone else working with me can do?* Once you identify those things, empower others to do them so you can pursue some of your other interests.

3. REST

Make room for meditation in your rest time. Make sure that the activity of your life is free from striving, free from demands or schedule pressures, free from personal performance expectations, and free from a results-producing focus. That may sound like hard work. Learn to read for enjoyment, stimulation, and revelation. Reflect on God's Word and meditate on the many ways it applies to the circumstances of your life and family (see Joshua 1:8).

4. RESTRUCTURE

Your understanding of Sabbath needs a gracious rather than legalistic structure. Without a plan, God has nothing to work with, and the benefits He offers through rest will be robbed from you. Without a plan to help you with the pace of your life and the rhythm of your commitments, you will react to things that come up or follow the whims of the day. These are my suggestions for restructuring your work and rest:

- Make a list of things that interest you.
- Prioritize the items on the list from most to least important.
- Schedule that list into a daily plan.

Make sure you consider your upcoming demands and commitments. Allow time for preparation that will fit the rhythm of your life so you can avoid the frantic pace of last minute preparations.

I will close this lesson with one final thought about living your life in a godly rhythm. The seasons of our lives and the demands within those seasons will change. I personally believe that a season is usually an approximate seven-year cycle. That timeframe should not make you think you can simply set things in motion to manage the energy grid of your life and enjoy Sabbath. You can't assume that once you set a pace, you can just leave it on autopilot. What works in one season may have to be adjusted in a new season for it to remain effective. If you set the rhythm of your life in motion on an effective path and then neglect to manage the things I have discussed in this lesson, then you will find that the energy grid of your life has become overloaded. You may end up wondering what happened or why it isn't working. Your life will not stay in rhythm nor with a lifegiving pace unless you are diligent and pay constant attention to the ways you use your energy.

> Since therefore it remains for some to enter it, and those who formerly received the good news failed to enter because of disobedience, again he appoints a certain day, "Today," saying through David so long afterward, in the words already quoted,
>   "Today, if you hear his voice,
>   do not harden your hearts."
>
> —Hebrews 4:6–7

Lesson 11

SEEK OUT AND EMBRACE WHAT IS TRUE.

For the law was given through Moses; grace and truth came through Jesus Christ.

—John 1:17

If you abide in my word, you are truly my disciples, and you will know the truth, and the truth will set you free.

—John 8:31–32

This is the message we have heard from him and proclaim to you, that God is light, and in him is no darkness at all. If we say we have fellowship with him while we walk in darkness, we lie and do not practice the truth. But if we walk in the light, as he is in the light, we have fellowship with one another, and the blood of Jesus his Son cleanses us from all sin.

—1 John 1:5–7

WHEN I LIVED in Amarillo, one of my friends was involved in an accident and broke his foot. It was swollen, he couldn't put his weight on it, and he limped as he walked. When I saw him after the accident, I asked what happened to his foot. He responded, "Nothing" and claimed he was fine. Then he finished by delivering a religious platitude: "Praise the Lord, I am redeemed, highly favored, and walking in the promises of God." That's when I replied, "But you're limping. You can't get your shoe on your foot because it is so swollen. And you think nothing is wrong? It sure looks to me like something is wrong!"

Despite my friend's condition, he was standing firm on his perspective, denying the reality of his circumstances. But the truth, as I saw it, was that he had a broken foot. Recognizing that reality would not have kept the Lord from healing him. However, his perspective kept my friend from getting proper medical care as he suffered for six weeks waiting for his foot to heal. Meanwhile, he kept limping and continued to claim nothing was wrong.

In this lesson, I will discuss what is real and true. Faith, vision, and God's work do not reside outside or in opposition to truth and reality. Jesus said about Himself, "I am the way, the truth, and the life" (John 14:6). When we come to Him, it must be through the door of truth. That applies to us individually as well as to the work we do for Him in the ministries of the church.

Television shows and movies often portray a false reality that no one can achieve in real life. Many times they present an exaggerated view of life that is bigger, more grandiose, and often better or worse than reality. In real life people actually have to leave the coffee shop and go to their jobs. When they get shot, they often die from their wounds. They have to live with the decisions made by others who didn't ask for their opinions. Instead, they are left with the results of those decisions, which often have life-altering consequences.

Denial is the blindfold that keeps us from seeing life's events from an honest point of view. God will always tell us the truth with tones of love and a heart of commitment. Denial, however, will move you down the road with unaddressed emotional and spiritual baggage in your trunk. Don't allow denial to ride along with you by creating a false sense of peace and happiness in your service to God. Seek friends and mentors who will help you find and live in the truth. Choose those who will not enable you to live in denial. In the apostle John's first epistle, believers are told about the importance of walking in truth. The truth of God's Word is a light on the path for our feet to follow. John declares,

> God is light, and in him is no darkness at all. If we say we have fellowship with him while we walk in darkness, we lie and do not practice the truth. But if we walk in the light, as he is in the light, we have fellowship with one another, and the blood of Jesus his Son cleanses us from all sin (1 John 1:5–7).

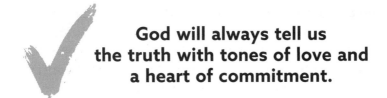

God will always tell us the truth with tones of love and a heart of commitment.

THREE CATEGORIES OF PEOPLE WE ENCOUNTER

In his book *Necessary Endings*, Dr. Henry Cloud, a best-selling author and clinical psychologist, says there are three kinds of people we will encounter as we walk through life—the wise, the foolish, and the evil. He writes, "Different people, in different categories, require different strategies."[1] Dr. Cloud qualifies these category classifications by saying they are not intended to force people into descriptive boxes that become straitjackets to prevent them from expressing themselves in a healthy way. These are also not judgments to declare that individuals have characteristics that can't be changed. Rather, these categories are appraisals of individuals' current

---

1. Henry Cloud, *Necessary Endings* (New York: Harper Collins, 2010), 122.

conditions and how they are relating to people in the circumstances of life and work. I believe these categories also reflect the way people relate to truth. They will embrace it, deny it, or reject it.

The Bible says we should use appraisals such as these to guide us in the way we interact with and relate to people. We must not use these appraisals to judge others. Dr. Cloud's three descriptive categories relate to the fruit that truth produces in our lives. The wise embrace truth, the foolish deny it, and the evil reject it. Every person, to some degree, has lived according to all three of these positions at one point or another.

THE WISE PERSON

Wise people embrace truth and live in the light of God's Word. When they are corrected, they receive that correction and change in response. They will even thank the person who is correcting them for loving them enough to tell them the truth.

How do you lead a wise person? You do it by giving advice supplemented with loving correction. You withhold none of your experience from wise people because they will listen to you. You coach, give feedback, and provide resources as you act as a mentor. With wise people, you don't question whether it is worth the investment of your time to interact with them. You know your investment will produce great fruit because they will listen and incorporate what you have to say to them.

**With wise people,
you don't question whether
it is worth the investment of
your time to interact with them.**

The input you give to a wise person will relate to values, culture, and mission. These are the elements that determine the chemistry within your team and influence the atmosphere around it. When you consider the investment of your time, you want to devote it to individuals who are wise and whose values will complement the team as a whole. You must make sure their values match your culture before you give them a significant place in your life, because they will influence the entire organization. The wise person needs appropriate feedback, directional coaching, and relational empowerment, which then challenges them to produce and succeed. When their values align with yours, the culture will be enriched and the mission advanced. The time you invest will be satisfying, easy, and fun.

THE FOOLISH PERSON

A foolish person can be very bright and gifted yet difficult to lead. The gifts of foolish people have led them to places of influence and possibly even to positions of importance. They produce results for the organization, but at what cost? They are relationally difficult people. They resist input and deny the impact of their actions. They support things that represent their agenda, yet they struggle to reflect the vison and values of the organization that differ from their own. The success of foolish people makes them vulnerable to expressions of arrogance, pride, and stubbornness, which then create tension with other members of the team.

When wise people see the light of truth, they adjust their behavior to fall in line with the direction given to them. Not so with the foolish. They respond to the light of truth by shielding their perspective to keep the light from hurting their eyes. Their physical response is akin to an allergic reaction—they break out with a rash of emotions and hives of resistance. Foolish people will become uncomfortable and irritable, all the while denying any culpability in what went wrong. Ultimately, they don't embrace what is being said to them. They attempt to dim the light of revelation while they look for an emotional "EpiPen" to counteract their discomfort. They either deny reality, or they try to adjust to the truth without embracing it in a way that will lead to positive change. The wise man changes himself, but the foolish man changes the truth.

Foolish people try to minimize the importance of the direction they receive by saying things such as, "You're making a lot out of a little" or "It's not like that at all"—even though you know it is exactly like that. They will suppress, deny, or eliminate the truth once they are exposed. Whenever you give feedback to a person and the response is reactive, defensive, resistive, or laced with denial, let that be a warning sign. Their defensiveness is equivalent to squinting their eyes to filter out the light of the truth you are giving them.

Foolish people create an environment of hopelessness. You may wonder why you do not look forward to meetings with them. If you stop long enough to evaluate your feelings, then you will recognize that you feel hopeless to influence them with your input or oversight. When you become hopeless in relating to a person, feeling that you will not be able to effect change in them, then recognize as a leader that it is time to change your approach and take correction to a new level.

You may have initially approached someone and thought, *We will work well together. I will be their mentor, and who knows? We may even become friends!* You expected they would embrace your correction as an overseer and listen to your directives. You thought they would change their behavior with your input, but their reactions have indicated something quite different. You now realize that they've never really listened to you and they have their own agenda.

When this kind of hopelessness begins to rise up within you, it is an indicator that your interaction must change from coaching to correcting. Your motive must now be to protect the group as a whole rather than simply helping this one individual. Your caring for them doesn't change; rather, it shifts its emphasis to address and limit the impact of foolishness on your team and the organization as a whole.

Research confirms what the Bible reveals: when you talk to a wise person, they will love you for it, listen, and get better. But the Bible strikes a different note when we encounter fools:

> Do not speak in the hearing of a fool,
>> For he will despise the good sense of your words
>> (Proverbs 23:9).

Many Scriptures describe the reality of responses from a foolish person (see Psalm 92:6; Proverbs 10:14, 23; 12:15; 13:16; 17:10, 12; 26:10; 27:22; 29:9). You may be experiencing these types of responses and not know how to address them. The Bible provides the proper strategy for dealing with a fool, and that is to stop talking. Why does the Bible give this advice? Because a foolish person has already stopped listening. Their "allergic" reaction (with all its unhealthy symptoms) is now in charge and in control of their responses. It's your responsibility as a leader to take authority over this foolishness, stop the insanity, and protect everyone else who is being influenced or impacted by it.

If you have to take this approach, Dr. Cloud gives the following example of a conversation starter:

> Joe, I have talked to you about *a*, *b*, or *c* on several occasions, and I do not want to talk about those anymore. It is not helping. What I want to talk about now is a different problem. The problem that I want to talk about is that trying to talk to you about a problem does not help. So what would you

suggest we do about that? How can I give you feedback so that you will listen to it and do something about it?[2]

This shifts your input from coaching about their behavior to a discussion that identifies their choices for moving forward. Your talk may take such a serious tone that a breakthrough in understanding will occur and the foolish person will make the necessary changes. If that happens, then you may not need to let them go but can shift them to a different role in the organization with fewer responsibilities. However, you cannot continue with business as usual and keep them in the same role; it is time for a change.

If the foolish person refuses to change, then ask yourself if it is time to transition this person out of the organization. Maybe everything that has taken place has been a process of God's work to loosen them from their position so that both of you will be motivated to consider another assignment for them outside the organization. In this case, repositioning them in your organization will not solve the problem. It may take some time, but sooner or later, you will be back at this same place. A truthful conversation about what is best for the person and for the organization is what is needed.

Remember this: *fools don't change their behavior until the pain of not changing becomes greater than the pain associated with the change.* King Solomon revealed this truth:

> Foolishness *is* bound up in the heart of a child,
> The rod of correction will drive it far from him
> (Proverbs 22:15 NKJV).

To some degree, all of us are recovering fools. But the good news is that Jesus took our foolishness so we can live in His

---

2. Henry Cloud, *Necessary Endings*, 137.

wisdom and discover His destiny for our lives! The cure for foolishness is corrective discipline. By that, I mean discipline that is not vindictive or punitive but corrective. This type of discipline does not ignore or enable problems but addresses them head on. It redeems our gifts and focuses our actions toward the path of God's blessings and destiny.

The cure for foolishness is corrective discipline.

Your leadership challenge here is to know when you have offered the appropriate amount of corrective discipline. It is not easy to know when you have communicated enough to make it clear that things are not working and the consequences for someone's actions have led to a critical choice. When do you stop ignoring or denying that you are dealing with foolishness in a particular individual? Can you accept responses that are the equivalent of "one step forward and two steps back" by telling yourself that progress is being made? When is it time to have a conversation to discuss the options for change? How do you know when a transition is necessary?

These conversations are neither fun nor easy, but when the circumstances lead you to this point, you can't shrink from your responsibility. It may be uncomfortable and difficult, but the truth is your friend. Make your communication firm yet kind and use it as the catalyst that forces a choice. This is not the time to second guess or blame yourself. It is time for action. The conversation might go something like this:

> I don't seem to be getting through to you. It seems to me that you are not hearing me, or if you are hearing me, you are not

accepting what I am telling you. I don't think you're a bad person. On the contrary, you are definitely gifted. I just think you're not in the right place. Because your behavior isn't changing, we need to make a change for both of our good.

Then have the courage to walk out a transition that leads to radical change.

THE EVIL PERSON

An evil person attempts to advance their own agenda through accusation, resistance, and stonewalling. It may be difficult to imagine that a person has such intentionally evil motives that drive their behavior, but it is true. As we seek to live in the light of truth, we must be aware of the presence of evil, and we must resist it rather than ignore or deny it. There truly are bad people in the world. We do not fear them, but they are real. This truth speaks to the spiritual nature of the things we wrestle with in the everyday circumstances of our lives. I've seen this kind of evil surface in board meetings, private conversations, and high levels of leadership.

Evil always wants to bring division and relational conflict, which will then cause disunity. It will accuse motives and assassinate character as a means of deflecting scrutiny and avoiding personal introspection. Paul tells us to deal this way with an evil person:

> As for a person who stirs up division, after warning him once and then twice, have nothing more to do with him, knowing that such a person is warped and sinful; he is self-condemned (Titus 3:10–11).

If we identify a person in this category, then protection becomes our major concern. An evil person will do more than resist your input. They will actively work against what you are doing because it does not serve their agenda. They will stir up discord and strife. This kind of behavior acts like cancer. If allowed to metastasize in any area of the organization, then it will rob life from the people and destroy your mission.

Be aware that evil people may be among your high-level leaders and volunteers, as well as members of your staff. A person who falls into the evil category will use the platform of the organization to promote their own agenda through division, strife, accusations regarding motives, and resistance to authority. They will work every angle to use their role, responsibilities, and authority for their personal advantage. They will attempt to represent their own culture, values, and mission rather than embracing those of the organization. To an evil person, the only satisfying result is to do things their way.

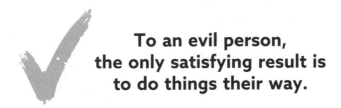

To an evil person, the only satisfying result is to do things their way.

The process of uncovering an evil person begins with discussions that attempt to answer their questions and understand and incorporate their perspectives. However, when these conversations result in arguments and resistance, the person must be told to cease and desist. They must be instructed to stop their maneuvering in an attempt to gather people to their perspective. They must be ordered to stop their factious conduct and clearly warned that if their behavior does not show swift and significant improvement, the result will be their removal from your organization as a staff member, leader, or even as a volunteer. They will no longer be welcome to participate in any of your events.

Does this seem harsh? It really is not; it is actually loving. You simply cannot allow one person's rogue agenda or character to stir up disunity and stop the mission God has given to your organization. You will not address the situation in meanness, spite, or with unkind words. It will be done with the authority of leadership that is equally as firm as it is kind.

It usually makes us feel better to think we are always wise. However, no matter how much wisdom we possess, the ability to act foolishly or with evil motives remains in us. We make foolish decisions when we try to change or minimalize the truth. Even worse, we can refuse to accept the truth and become a source of conflict and division. We must constantly guard against foolish and evil behaviors so they do not become defining patterns in our lives. If we want to be known for wise and godly behavior, then we must live in the light of God's truth. Ask yourself, *Am I walking in the light of God's Word? Am I seeking and embracing truth by walking in wisdom?*

> Whoever walks with the wise becomes wise,
>   but the companion of fools will suffer harm.
>
> —Proverbs 13:20

> The wise will inherit honor,
>   but fools get disgrace.
>
> —Proverbs 3:35

> Buy truth, and do not sell it;
>   buy wisdom, instruction, and understanding.
>
> —Proverbs 23:23

Lesson 12

BE NICE TO PEOPLE WHO ARE DIFFERENT.

A new commandment I give to you, that you love one another: just as I have loved you, you also are to love one another. By this all people will know that you are my disciples, if you have love for one another.

—John 13:34–35

Judge not, that you be not judged. For with the judgment you pronounce you will be judged, and with the measure you use it will be measured to you. Why do you see the speck that is in your brother's eye, but do not notice the log that is in your own eye? Or how can you say to your brother, "Let me take the speck out of your eye," when there is the log in your own eye?

—Matthew 7:1–4

EVERY PERSON HAS a story to tell. These are stories of the hurts, experiences, and circumstances that have shaped their development. For many people, their stories include the pain of selfishness and self-centeredness, which may go back for generations. These stories also include the ways God has been working to redeem them from the past and how He has led them into freedom and His divine purposes. Some people have not yet found Christ, so they are still living in the pain and bondage that reflect the brokenness of humanity without God's redeeming love.

We must be aware that God has made each person unique. No two people are exactly alike, and Christ died for each one of us. Although we may not want to admit it, every person has imperfections, idiosyncrasies, and behaviors that rub against the people around them. Our differences have various sources. Sometimes they are rooted in bitterness, judgments, and inner vows, which are the result of hurts we experience through life's events. We have all been bent in certain ways by the influence of our families as we developed into adults. Depending on the health of your family, you could be severely bent toward certain types of behavior. The circumstances of life and our reaction to them influence the individual people we become.

Through counseling people over the years, I have found that every person tends to think of their family experiences as normal and common. When I ask a person to tell me their story, they will often begin with a statement that goes something like this: "Well, I grew up in a normal family ...." Then they will start describing events from their childhood that reflect the hurt, pain, and dysfunction of broken humanity. They will share the circumstances that shaped them into the people they have become. These people come to counseling because they want to know why they are in emotional or spiritual pain. My role as a counselor is to help them see that they may be overlooking the influences that have shaped their lives.

You can't fully understand a person's behavior or thinking until you have walked a proverbial mile in their shoes. If you try to relate to them solely based on your own experiences, then you will miss the uniqueness of their story and its impact on who they have become as an adult. Seek understanding, extend grace, show compassion, and exhibit respect as you see that each person is different from you. Our differences can keep us from engaging with people the way God desires. Their pain may stem from the hate, discrimination, and rejection they have experienced that have nothing to do with you. However, their pain may also become a wall that separates them from you through an unwillingness to let down their guard and open up in a relationship.

When I was in the fifth grade, my best friend was Steve Naabidee. We were both in Indian Guides and did everything together at school. I would often ask him to come to my house to play, but I never wanted to go to his. I never considered the reason. He lived right across the street from the school, and it would have been easier to go to his house, but I preferred for him come to my house several blocks away. One day, Steve asked me if I would come with him to his house to eat lunch. We had 40 minutes for lunch and could go home if we lived close enough to the school. I remember that it was a huge dilemma for me. I wanted to go, but I also didn't want to go. Ultimately, I decided to go.

Years later I was married and living in Amarillo with two kids. I was struggling to accept some people who I thought were a little weird. They were certainly different from me, and I did not feel comfortable around them. For some reason I suddenly remembered my childhood friend and the feelings I had about being at his house. In that moment the Lord spoke to me about my attitude. He revealed that the root of what I was feeling is what caused me anxiety about going to my friend's house. I asked, "What root was that?" The Lord replied, "The root was difference. You are uncomfortable with people who are different from you."

I had to confess that what God was saying to me was true. It was easier for me to stay away from those who were different from me than it was to be around them and come to terms with the differences. I did not hate others for their differences—I simply didn't know how to deal with them. I did not realize that as I distanced myself from these people, I was also rejecting them. I did not know how to reconcile and accept those things that made us different.

If the world only contained people just like us, then it would be a very boring place. Individual uniqueness is what brings beauty, color, and spice into our lives. If you are like me and struggle with the "differences" that make it hard for you to accept and relate to people, then the Lord wants to help you just as He has helped me. He will give you grace, love, and compassion if you will ask Him. Then you will be able to accept and appreciate the differences of others. Through acceptance, appreciation, and respect, God will open the door for you to express love. You can't fully understand others if you are not willing to enter their world. Open your heart and mind to the reality that different does not mean "wrong." It may actually mean better. This is the humility God expects of us.

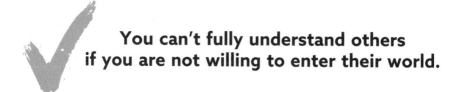

You can't fully understand others if you are not willing to enter their world.

There's a high likelihood that one day you will work for someone you don't fully understand, you will become friends with someone different than you, or you will even marry someone who is a little quirky but also needs what you can bring to the relationship. You will supply strength where the other person is deficient. If you hang back and avoid engaging with others because they are different, then you will miss opportunities to grow personally and impact the people around you.

God has ordained life to work in such a way that we are incomplete in our individual selves. If we reject others because we don't understand them, then we miss a big part of God's training and preparation for our lives. We need what others supply to make us complete. When you are connected with someone who is different from you, it is God's way of developing your character and ministry skills. He will smooth and polish your rough edges and teach you compassion and grace. You will learn by exploring and gaining understanding for what has made people different.

Remember, God loves everyone, and only He can fully understand what has made others into the individual people they are today. He knows their experiences, hurts, values, and gifts. If we are going to reflect His love for people, then we need to explore the elements that make them unique with curiosity, sensitivity, and grace.

THREE STEPS TO BREAK
THROUGH DIFFERENCES

How can you break through the resistance and overcome the feelings you have because of the differences between you and the people in your life? Here are three steps that will help you:

RECOGNIZE

Recognize your natural resistance to people who are different from you. Then repent for any negative thoughts or feelings you are holding on to and ask God for help. Fear is not from God. If you fear people or situations because they are outside your experience or comfort zone, then stop and recognize that fear. Admit it but don't accept it or adapt your life to it. Ask God to help you overcome that fear with His love. Break its stronghold over your life and watch God pour His love into the space that fear once occupied.

PUSH

Push through the discomfort you feel because of the differences. God will give you power to overcome your discomfort if you act in faith. Willingly step into settings that would normally cause you anxiety or stress because they are new and different. As you encounter new people and situations outside your experience, God will expand you. I am not saying you should put yourself in danger; however, don't let your fear of danger serve as an excuse when the situation isn't really dangerous. In that case, simply admit to God that you are uncomfortable, and He will help you. The danger we feel is often not physical but spiritual. That is because we are working with God to tear down strongholds so that we can experience something new and He can do a new work in us.

ACCEPT

Accept people who are different from you without judging them. Realize that as you accept them and their differences, it does not mean you agree or approve of everything that makes them different. Your acceptance of them is not an admission that you are wrong for the way you are, nor are you conceding that they are right for how they live and behave. You are simply accepting the reality of the differences. You are not required to give up your values, traditions, or your current way of doing something—at least not immediately. You may realize over time that something in you does need to change. At first, however, you are acknowledging the other person's experiences and extending compassion and care for the hurt and dysfunction they may have experienced. By your acceptance, you validate the other person as an individual of great value. Embracing this important point will revolutionize your relationships. It will change the atmosphere around you and transform your relational dynamics as you interact with others on the basis of acceptance rather than holding them at an arm's length.

By your acceptance, you validate the other person as an individual of great value.

Don't allow yourself to use pejorative terms like nerd, stupid, weird, or any other name that helps you justify your rejection of another person. Their differences do not give you the right to put them in a relational quarantine. You do not have to keep yourself away from them to make sure you are not infected with their differences. Paul put it this way:

> Love is patient and kind; love does not envy or boast; it is not arrogant or rude. It does not insist on its own way; it is not irritable or resentful; it does not rejoice at wrongdoing, but rejoices with the truth. Love bears all things, believes all things, hopes all things, endures all things. Love never ends. As for prophecies, they will pass away; as for tongues, they will cease; as for knowledge, it will pass away (1 Corinthians 13:4–8).

So be nice to people who are different from you! Remember, God loves them, He created them in His image, and Jesus died for them too.

> But they did not receive Him, because He was traveling toward Jerusalem. When His disciples James and John saw *this*, they said, "Lord, do You want us to command fire to

come down from heaven and consume them?" But He turned and rebuked them, [and said, "You do not know what kind of spirit you are of; for the Son of Man did not come to destroy men's lives, but to save them."]

—Luke 9:53–56 (NASB)

Lesson 13

YOU ARE EITHER AN INFLUENCE OR YOU'RE BEING INFLUENCED.

Do not be deceived: "Bad company ruins good morals."
—1 Corinthians 15:33

You are the salt of the earth, but if salt has lost its taste, how shall its saltiness be restored? It is no longer good for anything except to be thrown out and trampled under people's feet. You are the light of the world. A city set on a hill cannot be hidden. Nor do people light a lamp and put it under a basket, but on a stand, and it gives light to all in the house. In the same way, let your light shine before others, so that they may see your good works and give glory to your Father who is in heaven.
—Matthew 5:13–16

Train up a child in the way he should go;
    even when he is old he will not depart from it.
—Proverbs 22:6

You shall teach them diligently to your children, and shall talk of them when you sit in your house, and when you walk by the way, and when you lie down, and when you rise.
—Deuteronomy 6:7

I ONCE HEARD a corporate recruiter of top-level executives say he used a system when interviewing candidates for his clients. He would engage in light conversation with the candidates so they would become comfortable, even to the point of loosening their ties or removing their jackets. As soon as he felt they had let their guard down, he would lean forward with a very serious look and ask, "What is your purpose?" Without fail, he would catch them off guard, and each of these highly skilled, experienced, and successful leaders would struggle to find an answer. That is, until one candidate's response shocked him and changed the game.

The recruiter followed the normal process, got the recruit to let down his guard, and then popped the usual question. However, this recruit leaned in with confidence and threw him for a loop with this response: "My purpose in life is to go to heaven and take as many people with me as I can!" After answering the question, the recruit sat confidently back in his chair—calm, cool, and collected—as if to say, "What do you think of that?!" The recruiter was amazed. No other candidate had ever been that quick, confident, or articulate in answering that question.

What if I were to ask you the same question? Do you know the purpose for your life? Could you give a clear, unwavering statement to someone who asked? In other words, do you really know what you stand for? And do you know who you really are? These are fundamental and significant questions. At the heart of them reside your true character and a system of values upon which you make decisions and initiate actions. In our developmental years, our parents should guide us through a discovery process that will help us identify our interests, abilities, and passions. They use what they learn about us to then point and guide us along the path toward our purpose. Not everyone has experienced this guidance, but that is what God intends. How tragic it is for a person to go through life and achieve great wealth, influence, and status yet not be able to describe the purpose for which they have accumulated all these things. I find it so sad that many people are unable to connect their achievements to either a purpose or a divine calling.

> **How tragic it is for a person to go through life and achieve great wealth, influence, and status yet not be able to describe the purpose for which they have accumulated all these things.**

One of the foundational responsibilities of parents is to transfer their value system to their children. This value system should be framed around the recognition that God is our Creator and heavenly Father. Admittedly, this cannot really be done in a classroom setting, but it must be done intentionally. It cannot be accomplished by assigning a strict set of behavioral rules, which the parent then legalistically enforces upon the child. Rather, it is taught through behavioral modeling, gentle instruction, and consistent correction. Deuteronomy 6:7 describes the process by which parents should impart their values to their children. Parents are told to take advantage of these key times throughout the day:

- when they are at home
- when they are engaged in life's activities
- when they are putting their children to bed
- when they are beginning their day

Parents are commissioned to impart their values and monitor the way they are applied in their children's lives through real-life interactions and conversations throughout the day.

The living God intended for the dynamic relationship we have with Him to be introduced, modeled, and transferred through the loving, interactive, and involved mentoring of the parent to their child. All this work was to be accomplished within the context of belonging and connecting in the family. My parents, Jim and Joyce Lane, were married for 40 years. They had three children: Tom (me), Leslie, and Janet. We are the Lane family. I would not be able to tell you how many times my parents pointed out behaviors they observed in us or our friends that did not reflect the Lane family values. They would say, "We are Lanes, and Lanes don't do that!" My parents were demonstrating in real terms that there is value, identity, and connection in a name.

When I became a follower of Christ, imagine how easy it was for me to transfer what my parents had taught and modeled for me into my new family with God. I have a heavenly Father, and as the head of our family, He has values and principles that reflect His nature and character. It was so easy for me to hear in my heart, "You are in God's family now, and in God's family, we don't do that, we don't say that, and we don't act like that."

Additionally, it was easy for me to understand the importance and value of a good name. I learned that one of the greatest responsibilities of a family member is to represent the family and uphold its good name with your words and actions no matter where you go. As I read Paul's admonition to the Ephesians, I read it as a family value statement: "But sexual immorality and all impurity or covetousness must not even be named among you, as is proper among saints" (Ephesians 5:3). I know that it is related to our good name as followers of Christ.

As I continued to mature, my parents made it clear that they were monitoring the influence of my friends. How much impact would they have on my behavior? That was always the question my parents wanted answered. If my friends were doing something that I knew was wrong, would I join in or refuse to participate? Even more, would I boldly object, use my influence for what I knew was right, and point out what I knew my peers were doing wrong? If I could not stand against the pressure of a wrong influence from my friends, then my parents would limit my involvement with those friends. My mom and dad showed me how to recognize when the tug of my friends' influence was more than I could resist. I began to evaluate my friends' influence, distinguishing what they did for the good, the not so good, and the bad. I learned to determine what effect they had on my attitudes and behaviors.

When I left my parents' home, got married, and had my own children, I had a firm understanding of the importance of a good name. I remained aware of the ways others influenced my behavior, so I chose to spend my time with people who encouraged me to maintain positive thoughts, decisions, and actions. With the foundation my parents laid, I was able to establish my own parenting patterns that would help my children gain the same understanding of the people who were influencing their lives. I did my best to pass on what I had gained from my own mom and dad. I wanted to teach my children how to exert their own positive influence on those around them and how to measure the impact they received from their friends' influence.

The apostle Paul wrote, "Bad company ruins good morals" (1 Corinthians 15:33). I sought to help my children understand that this was true and would remain true all of their lives. When I was growing up, my parents often said, "If you lie down with dogs, you will wake up with fleas." They used this phrase to help me understand that bad habits would rub off on me if I became close friends with people who held lower values than our family did. I could be around people with different values; I just could not let them influence me, or else my behavior would become like theirs.

Good friends are to be highly treasured. They carry our values and encourage us to walk true to them when difficult times come upon us. They also encourage us not to quit or compromise. Every one of us needs support and encouragement, so make sure that when you embrace a group of friends, it is a group with the right values. You may think you can surround yourself with thieves and not follow their ways (becoming a thief yourself), but the impact of their influence will erode the strength of your values and lead you to compromise. You will wake up one day and not recognize the person you have become.

To reinforce this truth with my children when they left to hang out with friends, I would say to them, "Remember, you are either an influence, or you're being influenced. Be the influence tonight." Just in case some plans developed that would not represent our values or might jeopardize our good name, I wanted them to have that as a reminder. My kids always knew they had an "out" with me if the influence was too much for them. No matter how late or where they were, they could always call me, and I would come pick them up. I made sure they knew they always had a choice to opt out even if they were not the driver.

What about you? Are you being an influence or being influenced? God has called us as His sons and daughters to be influencers like "salt" in this world, seasoning and preserving what is good and right. He has called us to be "light," illuminating the path of right behavior to those around us who might themselves be in compromising situations. Are you hanging out with friends who support and reinforce your values? Do they respect the importance of a good name? Don't let people around you talk you into compromising your values or jeopardizing your good name. Stand strong and be an influence!

> Leave the presence of a fool,
>   for there you do not meet words of knowledge.
>   —Proverbs 14:7

Lesson 14

MAKE SPIRITUAL HYGIENE AS IMPORTANT AS PHYSICAL HYGIENE.

Put on then, as God's chosen ones, holy and beloved, compassionate hearts, kindness, humility, meekness, and patience, bearing with one another and, if one has a complaint against another, forgiving each other; as the Lord has forgiven you, so you also must forgive. And above all these put on love, which binds everything together in perfect harmony.

—Colossians 3:12–14

But thanks be to God, who in Christ always leads us in triumphal procession, and through us spreads the fragrance of the knowledge of him everywhere. For we are the aroma of Christ to God among those who are being saved and among those who are perishing, to one a fragrance from death to death, to the other a fragrance from life to life. Who is sufficient for these things?

—2 Corinthians 2:14–16

HAVE YOU EVER been seated next to someone on a bus or plane who did not practice good hygiene? Perhaps the spaces between their teeth were filled with food from their last meal. They had unwashed, unkept stringy hair. Maybe their body odor was a little more than your nose could handle. And you could tell they had neither bathed nor used deodorant within the last few days, which was a further assault to your olfactory system (i.e., they smelled really bad).

However, you may have also had compassion for them as you wondered what prevented them from caring for themselves in the right way. Their lack of hygiene was self-evident, but what you don't know is what tragic events brought them to this point. You know their current condition has very likely had a negative effect on their health and personal relationships since it is now having an effect on you. You also know that with a little effort, the right tools and cleaning products, and properly applied practices, this person could remedy many of the issues and improve their long-term health.

Did you know that spiritual hygiene has some similarities to physical hygiene? Some of us exhibit poor oral health in our spiritual lives. We haven't brushed off the influence of the flesh and the world around us for weeks, and it is evident to others as they listen to our words and feel the effects of our attitudes. We haven't regularly washed ourselves in God's Word, extended forgiveness to those who have offended us, or reoriented our behavior to the standards God expects. In the same way that people can detect the negative effects of poor physical hygiene, they also notice our poor spiritual hygiene. If we neglect the spiritual disciplines that help us maintain proper spiritual hygiene, then there is an odor coming from our lives that doesn't reflect God's work.

If we neglect the spiritual disciplines that help us maintain proper spiritual hygiene, then there is an odor coming from our lives that doesn't reflect God's work.

We practice physical hygiene to maintain good health and to present ourselves as acceptable to others. Our breath is important, and our body odor matters. The fragrance of our lives leaves a lasting impression, so most of us make a diligent effort to smell good and present ourselves in a positive way.

All this is true spiritually as well. The breath of God in you is the presence of the Holy Spirit activating God's Word through you. Make sure your language reflects the fragrant breath that comes from God's Word. Keep your words fresh smelling, positive, and redeeming rather than laced with old revelation, curses, or antidotes that carry stale odors from days past. Also, take the necessary care so your breath doesn't reflect the smell of worldly thinking or human-centered logic. Make sure your life doesn't give off the stench of bitterness or unforgiveness. Wear the fragrances of faith, humility, kindness, compassion, and generosity. These qualities will leave a sweet smell on you and give others a positive impression.

CONSISTENT SPIRITUAL HYGIENE

For many years, I have followed a morning physical hygiene routine. I get up from bed, go to the bathroom cabinet, and retrieve a basket that holds my hygiene products. I begin by flossing and brushing my teeth, and then I use my shaving cream and razor. I look for any unwanted hair around my face and trim any wayward hairs extending from my eyebrows. Then I move to the shower where I lather my hair with shampoo and thoroughly wash my body with soap. After I dry off with my towel, I return to the mirror to comb my hair and apply holding spray. I use deodorant, face cream, and cologne. Then I am off to my closet to dress. I put on fresh clothes, which are clean and pressed. Finally, I am ready for the day. I follow this routine in all kinds of weather every day, regardless of whether it is a holiday, weekend, or workday. My routine reflects my self-love and respect. The results also make a statement to others about me,

I believe my spiritual hygiene routine is just as significant as my physical one. That is why I make mental and spiritual cleanliness a priority. Every morning, I prepare myself for the day by leaving my house after I have completed my physical hygiene routine. You may not have to leave your home to maintain good spiritual hygiene, but that is how I do it. I need to go to a neutral place so I can keep my focus on the things I need in my spiritual life. If I stay home, I might be tempted to fall back asleep or get drawn into other activities around the house. If I go to my office, I know I'll be distracted by work matters. So where do I go? McDonalds. *That's right, McDonalds.* Why do I go there? First, because they have locations everywhere, no matter where I travel. Second, because they are open early every morning.

When I get to McDonalds, I order breakfast, open my computer to my favorite Bible software, access a prayer journal document saved on my desktop, and put in my wireless earbuds so I can listen to music. Then I meet with God. I read and meditate on His Word, talk with Him, and listen as He speaks to me. I focus on a particular verse or passage from my Scripture reading for the day, which will inspire what I write in my prayer journal. As Jesus' follower, I want to pray the way He instructed us to pray. I follow a pattern that I have drawn from the prayer the Lord taught His disciples in Matthew 6:9–13.

1. PRAISE AND SURRENDER

Psalm 100:4 tells us to enter the Lord's gates with thanksgiving and His courts with praise. Jesus said in Matthew 16:24 that we are to take up our cross and follow Him. I make it my practice to tell the Lord each day that I surrender to Him again, afresh and new. I yield to His leading and lordship in my life. I don't always express this surrender in the same way or with the same words, but my heart is always the same. It is bowed in His presence in complete surrender to Him and eager for His direction for me that day.

2. COMMITMENT AND ALIGNMENT

Samuel delivered an important truth to the disobedient King Saul: "To obey is better than sacrifice" (1 Samuel 15:22). As Christ followers, we must diligently seek to know and do God's will in our lives so we can be in line with His Kingdom's work. How do we diligently seek His will? In my quiet time, I tell God I want to obey Him and know and do His will. The apostle Paul tells us that God will work in us to do His good pleasure (Philippians 2:13). So I ask the Lord to align my heart, soul, mind, and body with His will. I commit myself to doing His will as He reveals it to me. If I have questions about what I think God is asking of me, then I go to trusted spiritual mentors and advisors to help me get clarity and direction.

As Christ followers, we must diligently seek to know and do God's will in our lives so we can be in line with His Kingdom's work.

3. NEEDS, CONCERNS, REPENTANCE, AND FORGIVENESS

When my children were young, they would ask me as their father for the things they wanted and needed. In the same way, I go to God as my Father and unashamedly bring to Him what

I want, what I feel I need, and what I am concerned about. And then I trust Him to do what is best with my requests. I think about difficult situations and people who have offended me and bring them to my Father. I ask Him to help me forgive others and to reveal my part in the problem. Then I repent and make things right with God and others. I recognize that if I don't forgive, then I won't be forgiven (see Matthew 6:14–15).

4. BLESSING AND VICTORY

God has called us to be a Kingdom of priests (see Isaiah 61:6; 1 Peter 2:5–9; Revelation 1:6; 5:10; 20:6). As such, we should pray blessings over our people. I am the priest of my home, so I regularly pray blessings over it using the pattern of Numbers 6:24–26. I pray for blessing, safety, provision, grace, God's abiding presence, and His peace and rest over my wife, our marriage, our children, and our grandchildren. I ask the Lord to assign angelic guards to accompany us in all our activities. I also ask Him to assist us in overcoming temptations and to give us victory over the schemes that the enemy tries to set against us each day.

5. PEACE AND REST

I pray for God's peace and rest to be upon our lives and for us to live in His favor. Psalm 23 ends with this statement: "Surely goodness and mercy shall follow me all the days of my life" (v. 6). The reason they will follow us is because Jesus is our Shepherd, we are His sheep, and we yield our lives to His care.

Rarely do I miss a day practicing both physical and spiritual hygiene. If I miss one, then I can feel the effects, and I can't wait to get back into my routine. No one has to force me to practice my hygiene regimens, because they are part of my daily habits

130

and disciplines. When I was young, my mom had to make me do what now has become second nature. She would remind me to brush my teeth and comb my hair before I left the house. She would ask if I had taken a shower after playing outside and sweating. Now that I am an adult, those physical hygiene practices are fully engrained into my behavioral pattern. I can proudly say that my wife rarely has to point out that I missed my hygiene for the day. I have taken responsibility for that part of my life.

When I first became a Christ follower, I had friends and mentors who became a part of my spiritual development. They would remind me to maintain my spiritual hygiene routine. They knew me well enough that they could tell when my spiritual odor wasn't clean and fresh. Now, having walked with Christ for more than 50 years, my spiritual hygiene routine is established just like my physical one. I have a process to ensure that I live clean and healthy, both physically and spiritually.

Make sure you don't leave your spiritual hygiene to chance or try to shoehorn it into your schedule. Be as diligent to maintain a clean heart, mind, and spirit as you do your physical body. Work to make sure that you present yourself as acceptable to God and to the people you will encounter in your day. This is part of taking responsibility for your spiritual life, and it reflects your maturing relationship as a Christ follower.

Have you matured to the place that you have taken responsibility for your spiritual hygiene? Do it with diligence. Let your aroma be sweet to others and to God.

> Who shall ascend the hill of the Lord?
>   And who shall stand in his holy place?
> He who has clean hands and a pure heart,
>   who does not lift up his soul to what is false
>   and does not swear deceitfully.

TESTED AND APPROVED

He will receive blessing from the Lord
   and righteousness from the God of his salvation.

—Psalm 24:3–5

Lesson 15

LIFE IS LIVED IN SEASONS, SO LEARN TO RECOGNIZE AND CELEBRATE THEIR COMING AND GOING.

The years of our life are seventy,
    or even by reason of strength eighty;
yet their span is but toil and trouble;
    they are soon gone, and we fly away.

—Psalm 90:10

For everything there is a season, and a time for every matter under heaven.

—Ecclesiastes 3:1

To make an apt answer is a joy to a man,
    and a word in season, how good it is!

—Proverbs 15:23

THE SEASONS OF LIFE

IF YOU LIVE in a region with clearly defined seasons, then you know all about the frustration, joy, or excited anticipation associated with seasonal changes. Many people who live

133

in areas with seasonal changes love and celebrate the beauty and distinct qualities of each season. However, if you live in an area with little seasonal change, then you may feel frustrated with the lack of variety, even though you may recognize slight changes from season to season.

God has also divided life into seasons. This is not a speculative claim; it is a scientifically verifiable fact. Our bodies, minds, and lives are all going through the processes of change. Our cells are changing all the time, but in approximately seven-year cycles, we go through radical transformations. Austrian philosopher Rudolf Steiner proposed the seven-year developmental cycle, which has been supported by other scientists. Steiner's work confirms a biblical view of the normal human life cycle. The Bible teaches that the normal human life is composed of 10 seven-year seasons, equaling a total of 70 years (see Psalm 90:10). If a human life is extended beyond 10 seasons, then it is because of strong genes and God's favor. Each season has a purpose for our physical, mental, and spiritual development.

The first three seasons (from 0–21 years) are *developmental and learning seasons.* The next two (from 22–35 years) *are discovery seasons.* People learn who they are, where best to apply their gifts, and with whom they will partner to fulfill the purposes of their lives. The next four (from 36–63 years) are *productive seasons.* People produce their reputations, heritages, wealth, and the impact their lives will have for the Lord. The tenth season (from 64–70 years) is for *celebration, reflection, and transfer. During this time,* people transfer their knowledge and resources to the next generation. The eleventh season and beyond is used for *reflection, mentoring, and preparation for transition into eternity.*

A wise servant of God understands and learns to embrace each of life's seasons. As one season comes to a close, don't hold on to it too tightly, or it will delay you from moving on to the next. Some people do not develop emotional, mental, spiritual, or even physical maturity because they get stuck in a particular season, and that is tragic. Each season has its own purpose, and when the time for transition comes, you will have an opportunity to reflect on its ending. Then you will be able to consider the joys, trials, and things you have learned and developed. You will celebrate and reflect on them, but you can't stay the same. You must change with the new season; you have to move on.

A wise servant of God understands and learns to embrace each of life's seasons.

Developmental seasons are especially designed to give you an awareness of your lifespan. During my teenage years and through my twenties, I did not consider that my life had an end. I didn't measure my life in seasons of seven years or in any other way. In other words, I did not think about my time on earth as a limited resource that is on a timer, rapidly ticking toward eternity. Only when you are aware of that progression can you invest your life's gifts and resources in the right ways, rather than squandering them on things that don't really matter. As the developmental seasons of my life have passed, I now realize how quickly they went by and how important it is for others to make the most of them. Each season is significant and important in your development and contributes to the growth of God's purposes in your life.

SIX SPIRITUAL SEASONS

In the same way we have developmental seasons in our lives, we also experience spiritual seasons. I have experienced at least six spiritual seasons in my life, and I would like to describe them for you.

THE DRY SEASON

In a dry season, it seems as though God is silent, or you don't hear Him as you once did. You have a feeling of distance between you and the Lord, despite your every effort to close the gap. In times like these, it is important for you to continue practicing what you know is right. Be faithful doing what you need to do, not because it feels good but because you are committed to being obedient to the Lord.

THE WAITING SEASON

After you have planted seeds and fertilized and watered them, you enter a waiting season in which you have yet to see the fruit of your labor. God's timing is not our timing, nor are His ways our ways (Isaiah 55:8–9). While you are waiting, God is working, and He wastes no time. With Him, everything has a purpose. You can relax and rest in faith, knowing He is behind the scenes causing the fruit you desire to grow. Wait patiently and trust in Him.

THE GRINDING SEASON

In a grinding season, you are processing, integrating, and building upon what God has given you in preparation for His expansion. This season is full of hard work, diligent application, and careful management of your pace. Do not neglect the

Sabbath as an excuse to work harder because you fear that the harvest of fruit rests solely on you. Remember to honor the Sabbath as both the command and gift of God.

THE TESTING SEASON

In a testing season, God is pressing you to see if you have learned and then applied what He has allowed you to be taught. God uses all testing to reveal His work and build our endurance. He does not test us to punish us. In fact, He will never test you so He can put the stamp of "failure" on your life. You will have big and little tests, including tests of your attitude and obedience. All God's tests are open book, so make sure you study and apply the Bible diligently in this season.

THE SPIRITUAL WARFARE SEASON

In a season of spiritual warfare, you may feel discouraged, oppressed, resisted, or defeated. The apostle Paul reminds us, "We do not wrestle against flesh and blood, but against ... the spiritual forces of evil in the heavenly places" (Ephesians 6:12). As a son or daughter of God, realize your work for Him will bring you face-to-face with the enemy's strongholds. In addition, the devil will probe the boundaries of your defenses to see if he can expose your vulnerabilities through temptations and accusations. Stand firm, raise the shield of faith, and fight with the sword of God's Word. Although Jesus defeated Satan, the devil still "prowls around like a roaring lion, seeking someone to devour" (1 Peter 5:8). Don't let him shake your faith; rather, trust God, resist the enemy, and you will overcome!

THE REJOICING SEASON

In a rejoicing season, you will experience great joy, thankfulness, and celebration for all that God has done. Although you will learn to praise God in every season, the rejoicing season is a special time for your heart to connect with God in joy and gratitude over all that He has allowed you to experience. In this season, you will find renewal and rest as you focus on the goodness of God.

A NEW SEASON IS COMING

If you find yourself in a tough season, facing trials and dealing with difficult situations, then don't fret or become resentful. Recognize it is a season, and a different one is on the way. Make the most of every season by learning all you can. In every season, there is productive work being done. You will carry the fruit of what you have learned and experienced into the next season. Some seasons are for resting, others for planting, and still others for harvesting. There are seasons for testing, seasons for building endurance and expanding your faithfulness, and seasons for rest and repair.

In every season, there is productive work being done.

Learn to recognize seasonal transformations by the signs of change. When the temperatures get cooler and the leaves on trees begin to change color, you know summer is ending and fall is coming. When an earthquake is about to happen, seismologists receive certain signs that warn them of impending movement under the ground that is about to come to the surface. These signs then become tremors, shakings, and violent quakes. It is important for you to recognize the signs of impending change so you can prepare for your transition into a new season. Spiritual seasons form outside your ability to control them in the same way earthly seasons do. You can't resist them; you can only recognize and prepare for them. Do your best to recognize them early so you will avoid the devastation that can happen when you have resisted and a season is forced upon you.

Finally, seasons have limited durations. When you are in a season, you may become weary from your current conditions, wondering if they will ever end. The enemy wants to rob you of the benefits of a season by getting you to focus on your feelings, the difficulty of the work, or the conditions you are experiencing. If he can get your focus on your discomfort, then he has an open line of attack to your thoughts. He will try to convince you that this season will be your last. He wants you to think you have arrived at God's purpose for your life and there is nothing left for you to do. He will try to tell you to get used to what you're experiencing because this is the way your life will be from now until you die. The devil's lies are designed to rob you of your faith and trust in God. Just as he did with Adam and Eve, the enemy will try to get you to act outside of God's timing and direction. Fight back against the devil's lies and remind yourself, *This is only a season. It won't last forever.* You may not know when, but this you can know for sure: it will pass. So don't let the devil bait you into giving up and compromising.

Do you know which season of life you are experiencing right now? What spiritual season are you in? Share your thoughts about them with a mature believer who is close to you. Ask that person to support you in your season. Then ask what season they are in and support them as well. Remember, no one can do life alone. We need one another. Each season is special, and God will use it for your development so you can always offer service that is pleasing to Him.

TESTED AND APPROVED

He is like a tree
    planted by streams of water
that yields its fruit in its season,
    and its leaf does not wither.
In all that he does, he prospers.

—Psalm 1:3

Lesson 16

DON'T TAKE UP AN OFFENSE, ESPECIALLY ONE THAT IS NOT YOUR OWN.

Good sense makes one slow to anger,
 and it is his glory to overlook an offense.

—Proverbs 19:11

Whoever covers an offense seeks love,
 but he who repeats a matter separates close friends.

—Proverbs 17:9

Keep your heart with all vigilance,
 for from it flow the springs of life.

—Proverbs 4:23

LET ME TAKE you back to where we began: "Ministry and life are not fair." In that first lesson, I wrote that we often define fairness by comparison, which means we compare our situation with that of another person. Then we declare they don't deserve more than us because we believe we have worked as hard or harder than them. Consequently, we think we deserve more, better, higher, longer, and bigger compared what they have gotten. If we don't get it, then we conclude, "It's just not fair." I want to remind you again that life isn't fair. Not only that, but at times it isn't just.

An injustice happens when someone is treated wrongly, taken advantage of, or violated in some way. When we experience injustice at the hands of other people, our instinct is to be offended, carry a grudge, or seek revenge. However, the correct response for believers is to forgive the injustice and trust God to make it right.

 **The correct response for believers is to forgive the injustice and trust God to make it right.**

When someone we know and love experiences an injustice that negatively affects them, it is hard not to become offended on their behalf (even if we didn't personally witness the wrongdoing). We have two instinctual responses when someone is treated wrongly: justice and comfort. These responses are inborn and developed when we are very young. For example, if one of our siblings snatched a toy from us, we would immediately respond with protest, or we might even hit the perpetrator for unjustly taking our toy. After that, we probably tattled to our parents and claimed that we were completely innocent in the altercation. We had been told not to hit our brother or sister, but we did it out of instinct, almost as a reflex.

Even if we were bystanders and not directly involved in the conflict, we still felt the temptation to come to the rescue and fight for the person we perceived as the "wronged" party. I have some experience with this kind of scenario. I have two younger sisters, and I remember times when I felt I had to step in and right an injustice. I would take a stolen toy right out of the

"guilty" sister's hands and return it to the one who originally
had it.

This instinct to make wrong things right is not something we
naturally grow out of as we become older. In fact, the United
States' legal system is based on ensuring and restoring justice.
The statue of Lady Justice stands outside the US Supreme
Court building and inside and outside of courthouses around
the world. With origins in Roman mythology, Lady Justice is
a blindfolded woman who holds the scales of justice, implying
that both equality and justice are blind to the status of any
particular individual or group. We believe justice should be
blind to privilege and status, and a legal system should apply
reasonable punishment or vindication based on the facts of an
individual case. Our sense of justice is satisfied when we believe
a wrong has been righted—and not until then. In contrast, we
find it exceedingly dissatisfying when our sense of justice is
either not met or completely overlooked.

We are all aware that the process of justice can become
perverted through corruption, bribes, deceit, and outright lies.
At times, the process to achieve justice takes longer than we
think it should; from our perspective, the injustice is clear, and
the facts are unquestionable. In contemporary society, we live
in an increasingly diverse culture with variant definitions of
justice. Without clear values or a common definition of right
and wrong, the process of obtaining justice becomes increasingly difficult and confusing. This moral chaos only adds to our
sense that justice is not satisfied.

Over the last four decades in the US, we have taken the
relativistic concept of "situation ethics" and embedded that
type of thinking into our schools, governmental institutions,
businesses, families, and, most remarkably, even our churches.
Principled people are seen as out of step with the rest of the
culture. Situation ethics and postmodern philosophy presume
that no single value system or definition of "truth" can be

accepted by a pluralistic society. Right and wrong are simply constructs of each individual's mind. There is no such thing as a "fact." Only the particular situation matters.

Whose values are most important in a relativistic culture? Yours are because they're yours. Is it wrong to hit your sibling? You have to consider the situation. Did they do something you didn't like? Then maybe it's not wrong. Every individual becomes a supreme court. Children may tell their parents they believe an injustice has been done to them, such as a teacher not treating them fairly. The parents respond with indignation without even checking the facts. It makes me wonder sometimes why anyone would want to become a teacher and subject themselves to that kind of treatment.

Those who fully embrace relativism and situation ethics do not believe that right and wrong are anchored in stable, unchanging truths and values. Relativism puts morality, ethics, and behavior on a sliding scale or even on shifting sands. Truth and values change based on the circumstantial details and fluctuating situations. If behavior is not based on a fixed system of right or wrong, then what is the deciding factor? For the most part, people base their values on changeable feelings or opinions. The person who makes the most persuasive or popular case is then considered "right."

As a result, true justice takes a back seat as our culture enables individuals to develop their own values. Our inborn, godly desire for justice goes unsatisfied while our emotions simmer, and we try to fight off the temptation to "go with the flow." We become angrier and more resentful as we see injustice, and we even become willing to adopt ungodly means to accomplish good ends. At worst, we explode with vigilante action in an attempt to right wrongs.

What do we do with our internal desire for justice in a world such as this? Do we make concessions to a relativistic moral structure because holding to our values is simply too exhausting? Do we construct our own individual definitions of justice? Not according to the Bible. In fact, Scripture tells us to trust in one system of justice—God's system. Only He is truly just, fair, and right. King David writes,

> God *is* a just judge,
> And God is angry *with the wicked* every day (Psalm 7:11 NKJV).

Moses said,

> *He is* the Rock, His work *is* perfect;
> For all His ways *are* justice,
> A God of truth and without injustice;
> righteous and upright *is* He" (Deuteronomy 32:4 NKJV).

The Bible also tells us that God is sovereign, and all authority rests in His hands (Romans 13:1). You can have absolute confidence in Jesus' judgment because He has the authority of God resident in Himself. In Matthew's gospel, a centurion approached Jesus and asked Him to heal his servant (see Matthew 8:5–13). Jesus was willing to go to his home, but the Roman soldier said Jesus could simply give the command and heal the servant. Jesus was amazed that the officer trusted God's spiritual system of authority, and He said, "Truly I tell you, with no one in Israel have I found such faith" (v. 10).

As a military officer, the centurion knew that authority comes from being under authority. He recognized that Jesus' authority came from being under the authority of God the Father. Therefore, the centurion understood that when Jesus spoke, God also spoke. He believed Jesus' word was enough to heal his servant.

God is a perfect judge, and because the Son is the exact representation of His Father, Jesus is also a perfect judge. Also, Jesus understands suffering. He experienced rejection, persecution, torture, and execution by crucifixion while in His human body. In a world full of injustice, we can take comfort knowing that it does not escape God's notice. We find relief in the knowledge that it is not our responsibility to extract a penalty for every injustice we experience or even observe; that is God's business. He has an unchanging standard in which *right is right* and *wrong is wrong,* and these don't slide based on circumstances. God will make every injustice right by grace through the blood of Jesus Christ in this life or through judgment at the end of the age. God is the eternal righteous judge.

Then what is our responsibility? It is to forgive as we have been forgiven. This truth is revealed in the prayer Jesus taught His disciples: "Forgive us our debts as we also have forgiven our debtors" (Matthew 6:12). Jesus illustrated this concept in the parable of the unforgiving servant (see Matthew 18:21–35). In this account, the servant begged a king to give him more time to gather money for a debt, which was an amount far greater than he could ever repay. The king showed mercy and forgave the entire debt. However, the servant then found a fellow servant who owed him a much smaller amount and demanded payment. The fellow servant asked for more time, but the first servant refused to show compassion and had the man thrown into prison until the debt was paid. News of this behavior soon reached the king. He rebuked the unforgiving servant and turned him over to the jailers until he could pay his debt in full. The debt was so large that he could never repay it, which meant he would spend the rest of his life in prison. Jesus concluded the parable by saying, "So also my heavenly Father will do to every one of you if you do not forgive your brother from your heart" (Matthew 18:35).

The parable of the unforgiving servant gives us a picture of the way God forgives our sins and how He expects us to forgive those who have sinned against us. He wants us to give up our "right" to extract our own justice for the wrongs done to us. Like the servant with a debt greater than he could ever repay, we too have been relieved of the penalty for the wrongs we have done against others and against God. How then can we not forgive the wrongs done to us? We must choose to walk in forgiveness. Our choice ultimately comes down to a matter of trust. Will we trust God to bring justice for the injustices we have experienced? Can we acknowledge that He alone determines how to right wrongs? Forgiveness is not an option; it is a command. You will not find an instance of God blessing someone for taking up another person's offense. The person who is wronged must forgive, and those who are close to them are not to take up offenses on their behalf.

Forgiveness is not an option; it is a command.

If a wrong is not actually perpetrated against you but hurts or damages someone you love, then you will be tempted to react. You may become angry with the person who caused the pain and feel the need to take actions on behalf of the injured party. How many relationships have been broken and social media fires set ablaze with accusations and hateful words because someone felt the need to defend a friend or loved one?

But that is not God's will for His people. I have never found a single Bible verse in which God encouraged a person to take up someone else's offense or gave them permission to impose their own form of justice. So what are you to do then? Do you stand on the sidelines and watch the hurt continue? No, not at all. When you observe a wrong being done, stand against the injustice and become a voice to give God's perspective on the matter. Offer sound, biblical advice and encouragement. But don't take up the offense. If you don't know what your response should be, then pray. You will discover the appropriate response through self-reflection and prayer, which will lead you to an obedient act of faith and not an act of retaliation. When you retaliate, you step into the place of judgment that belongs only to God, and you open your own heart up for a bitter root to take hold. Taking matters into your own hands will not produce godly fruit! Instead, you open yourself for stern discipline from God.

Wrong actions and responses are the fuse that lead to devastating church splits and fractured relationships. People watch these explosions happen in their extended families, among their friends, and with their coworkers, all of whom say they love each other and God. Worst of all, witnesses conclude that if this is what God is all about, then they are not interested. They are turned off by the vicious actions of Christians.

As followers of Christ, we are called to love. We must avoid holding grudges and taking up the offenses of others. We must choose to walk in love and forgiveness toward people and trust God to bring about justice for every wrong.

> The one who states his case first seems right,
>   until the other comes and examines him.
>   —Proverbs 18:17

Lesson 17

RESPECT AND APPRECIATE THE PLATFORM YOU HAVE BEEN GIVEN.

Do you see a man skillful in his work?
   He will stand before kings;
   he will not stand before obscure men.
                                                    —Proverbs 22:29

Likewise, you who are younger, be subject to the elders. Clothe yourselves, all of you, with humility toward one another, for "God opposes the proud but gives grace to the humble." Humble yourselves, therefore, under the mighty hand of God so that at the proper time he may exalt you.
                                                    —1 Peter 5:5–6

STRATEGIC PEOPLE UNDERSTAND the importance of the platform of influence. Marketers work to establish their "brand" as a means of influencing people. At Gateway Church, when we train our pastors or our worship team, we call the place of their presentation a "platform" rather than a "stage." We explain to them that a stage is for performance, but a platform is for influence. Ministry is about influence, not performance. We take great care not to confuse the two.

God calls us to conduct our lives in such a way that we will influence people toward Him (Matthew 5:16). He puts us in positions of service to people, and in the process, He uses our service to establish a platform of influence. Our integrity, our character, and our behavior determine our reputation. King Solomon wrote,

> A good name is to be chosen rather than great riches,
>   and favor is better than silver or gold (Proverbs 22:1).

Your reputation is associated with your name, and you must work hard to live in such a way that your reputation is worthy of the platform of influence you are given.

People often mistakenly believe that they can determine the size and scope of their influence. This is performance-based thinking. The truth is, the platform of our influence belongs to God, and He determines how big it will be—not us. In Luke 17:7–10, Jesus told His disciples that servants don't fulfill their responsibilities to be thanked or noticed; they fulfill their responsibilities because that is their duty. When it comes to the platform of our influence, we don't earn it; rather, God gives it to us. Keeping this mindset will help you walk in humility and appreciation for God's graciousness toward you. It will keep you aware that since He gave it to you, He can also take it away.

The platform of our influence belongs to God, and He determines how big it will be—not us.

Team ministry places multiple individuals on the same platform of influence. It's not a competition, but it is a collaboration for effective impact and the advancement of God's

Kingdom purposes. God appoints a leader to oversee the team, and that leader is supported by a responsible structure, which helps him steward the platform God has entrusted to him and the team. God gives and expands our influence in response to our obedience and faithfulness. Avoid the temptation to promote yourself and choose to trust God for your promotion as He sees fit. Be diligent, thankful, and respectful of the platform you have been given and steward it well.

In Acts 8, Luke gives the account of Simon the magician. Simon practiced magic in the city of Samaria and declared himself to be great. Citizens of the city, from the least to the greatest, all paid attention to him. Life was very good for Simon until Philip shared the gospel, and many in Samaria became Christ followers, including Simon. Simon was very impressed by the signs and miracles that followed Philip's ministry and the influence they gave Philip in the city. Peter and John soon followed Philip to Samaria and prayed for the new believers to receive the Holy Spirit. When Simon saw that the Holy Spirit was given to people when the apostles laid their hands on them, he offered Peter and John money to give him the power to impart the Holy Spirit just as they did. Simon was trying to buy their expression of influence. Peter's response was quick and firm: "Your money perish with you, because you thought that the gift of God could be purchased with money!" (v. 20). The apostles knew it is God who gives influence and platform; it can't be earned or bought.

God gives gifts to be used for His ministry and service to people. Gifted people will often impress others and draw their attention. When these gifted people presume that their gifts are enough to establish the platform of their influence, they fail to acknowledge God's sovereign authority. Only He can bestow gifts and His influence in the ways He determines. If we fail to recognize God's sovereignty, then we will think our gifts belong to us, and we will develop them for our own glory and influence.

When we use our gifts for personal gain, we have fallen prey to the same deception that plagued Simon. Even worse, this is the same attitude that led Lucifer to think he could establish his own platform of influence apart from God and God's work through him.

Your gifts will open a door of influence for you, but they can't sustain that influence on their own. God is the one who grants favor and determines our impact by providing the platform that sustains the influence of our gifts. I strongly advise you to stay clear of self-promotion of any kind. Learn to nurture contentment regardless of the size of your platform of influence. The apostle Paul wrote, "Whatever you do, work heartily as for the Lord and not for men" (Colossians 3:23), and he told Timothy, "Godliness with contentment is great gain" (1 Timothy 6:6).

For some people, wealth becomes an expression of their platform of influence. By building wealth, they build their influence. However, we must be careful not to allow anything, include wealth, distract us from God's calling on our lives. Paul cautions believers, "Those who desire to be rich fall into temptation, into a snare, into many senseless and harmful desires that plunge people into ruin and destruction" (1 Timothy 6:9).

If you wrongly assume the responsibility to build your own platform of influence, then you unwittingly take on the pressure to perform. Building influence by our own efforts still takes work and time, but it can tempt us to take shortcuts to produce the influence we desire. According to Isaiah 55:8, God's thoughts are not our thoughts and His ways are not our ways. Solomon wrote,

> Whoever is slothful will not roast his game,
>> but the diligent man will get precious wealth
>> (Proverbs 12:27).

152

As I mentioned in Lesson 9, people in Solomon's day couldn't go to a grocery store or market to get all of their food. They often had to hunt, or else they would not eat. When a hunter caught an animal, he had to clean and cook it before it was ready to eat. A diligent hunter would follow all the necessary steps before he ate, but a lazy man couldn't wait. He would take shortcuts to get to the results he desired, even eating uncooked meat in the field.

Are you trying to build your own platform of influence? Or are you trusting the Lord to build it for you? Is your character worthy? Is your reputation known and respected? The answers to these questions will determine the size of the platform of influence God will give you. Respect God's work and appreciate the platform you have been given. Give Him thanks and steward it well.

Whatever you do, work heartily, as for the Lord and not for men, knowing that from the Lord you will receive the inheritance as your reward. You are serving the Lord Christ.
—Colossians 3:23

Lesson 18

LOVE IS COURAGEOUS, YET IT DOES NOT ENABLE.

Love is patient and kind; love does not envy or boast; it is not arrogant or rude. It does not insist on its own way; it is not irritable or resentful; it does not rejoice at wrongdoing but rejoices with the truth. Love bears all things, believes all things, hopes all things, endures all things. Love never ends.

—1 Corinthians 13:4–8

A friend loves at all times,
and a brother is born for adversity.

—Proverbs 17:17

DURING MY FIRST few years in ministry at Trinity Fellowship Church, my friend Garvin McCarrell joined the staff as the youth pastor. In one of our first oversight meetings, Garvin asked me to make a commitment to him as a friend. I said, "Sure! Whatever you need, I am in." He said, "If I ever become ineffective in ministry and don't realize it, I want you to tell me. Will you promise me you will do that for me?" I replied, "Of course," and then I asked him to do the same for me, to which he agreed.

Ten years together went by really fast. The church grew steadily, and the demands of the expanding ministry and growing numbers of people kept us all busy. In an oversight meeting one day, Garvin said to me, "Hey, you're not keeping your promise!" I had no idea what he was talking about; from my perspective, he was very effective with the teenagers of our church. Nevertheless, he reminded me, "You promised you would tell me if I started losing my effectiveness in ministry!" I said, "Yes, I did say that, and I will." He responded, "I am losing my effectiveness, and you're not telling me."

That day we talked very openly. I explained to Garvin why I felt he was doing a great job. He confided in me why he felt he was losing his effectiveness. As I shared my perspective, it seemed to settle and encourage him. He left my office with a renewed attitude toward his role with the teens.

That heart-to-heart talk worked for a short time, but just six or eight weeks later, Garvin began expressing his feelings of ineffectiveness again. He asked me why I wasn't talking to him about it. He felt he was failing, and I was ignoring it. Once again, I told him I didn't see things the same way he did. But this time, it didn't comfort him. In fact, he seemed more unsettled. So I told him I would talk to our senior pastor (our boss) and get back to him with a response about what we would do. That answer seemed to bring him comfort and settled him with a resolve that something would be done.

It was springtime, and graduation exercises were coming, followed by summer camps. Garvin was looking for direction for his life and didn't feel youth ministry was where he needed to be. He said he was willing to step out of ministry and return to business if that was what we decided. He just couldn't stay where he was any longer. Garvin believed it was only a matter of time before his ineffective leadership would produce failure, which would then be noticeable to everyone.

In my oversight meeting with our senior pastor, Jimmy Evans, I told him about both conversations with Garvin and how he was expressing growing feelings of unrest. I asked

Jimmy for his insight and direction. He said, "Tell Garvin that by the end of June, he will be done with youth ministry." I thought, *Wow, that was quick and decisive.* I asked, "What do I tell him he will be doing?" Jimmy replied, "I don't know, but it won't be youth ministry."

That has always been Jimmy's leadership style—clear and decisive. I preferred a little more clarity and direction to pass along to Garvin, but Jimmy didn't yet have it to give. His decisive statement was all I got. In my next oversight meeting with Garvin, I relayed just what Jimmy had said. To my surprise, Garvin seemed satisfied with simply knowing he would not be working with the youth in a couple of months. He was comforted, even though he did not know exactly where he would be in the near future.

I learned an important leadership lesson that day. It takes courage, along with faith, to love people in a decisive way that will give them direction. That does not mean we will have all the answers. In fact, most of the time, that direction can't include all the answers. As long as the direction we give has an attitude of love and care and comes out of a heart of commitment, it will be enough. We demonstrate our commitment through our daily interactions with people, and we add trust to the mix when we do what we say we will do. Sometimes it is easy to keep our word, but we really build trust when it is hard and costs us more than we expect. Over time, our word becomes our bond and provides deep connections with the people we love, oversee, and to whom we minister.

It takes courage, along with faith, to love people in a decisive way that will give them direction.

When I relayed that direction to Garvin, we had no open positions on our staff, and I did not know of any transitions in the near future that would provide him with another spot. I did not tell him that, though, because he did not need to know that information. All he needed to know was that he wouldn't be leading the youth by the end of June. He trusted God (and us) to make a way if it was supposed to be with us, and if not, then God would use us to guide him in the way he should go. That trust is what settled him.

Before the end of June, an opportunity opened that had not been available when we first talked. It was the perfect fit for Garvin. He moved into that role and continued serving at Trinity Fellowship for almost twenty years. Then he took an assignment as an executive pastor with Pastor Brady Body at New Life Church in Colorado Springs.

Courage is strength in the face of pain or grief. When we love someone, it may seem counterintuitive to tell them something that will hurt their feelings (even if it's true). However, in reality, love is supposed to act with courage on their behalf and tell them the truth.

Courage is strength in the face of pain or grief.

I once received a call from the father of a young lady who worked in Gateway Church's children's ministry. She was assigned to special needs kids in the children's ministry, and she was very effective. Nevertheless, she was difficult to oversee, and the other workers did not enjoy working alongside her. She had to step away from the children's ministry for a few months due to an illness, and in her absence, a new peace settled over the children's ministry.

When this young lady called to say she was ready to return to work and wanted to be placed on the schedule, she was shocked and disappointed to learn there was no room for her and she had been replaced. This was especially upsetting because she had been told that her position would be held until she returned. The children's ministry team recommended that she try the church's youth ministry because they might have a place for her. However, she did not want to go to the youth ministry. She felt offended, brushed off, and frustrated.

After hearing about the situation, her father became angry. He called me to express his displeasure and wanted an explanation. At the time of his call, I was unaware that others felt his daughter had been a problem in the children's department. I also did not know about the decision to replace her or the attempt to pawn her off on the youth department. So I told the father that his report was the first I had heard about the situation. I asked him to allow me to do some investigation, and I promised I would get back to him.

I discussed the young woman's situation with the children's pastor, and he confirmed the story I had heard. He also gave me more details as to why she was given the brushoff. I asked him if she had been told the reason why her position had been given to someone else. He said she had not. Then I asked if she had been told that she created tension and discord among the people in the department. Again, he told me that this was not communicated to her. However, he did say there was full agreement with the team on the decision not to allow her to return. Although she did a good job and even was gifted with special needs children, she wasn't worth the drama and issues she created in the department. Consequently, they were happy not to have her return.

I understand that dealing with difficult people isn't easy, but I told the children's pastor that Gateway Church would not handle these types of situations in this manner. We confront with love and speak with honesty. I agreed to help this one time. I phoned the father and asked if he and his daughter would come to a meeting with me and the children's pastors so I could share some information. He agreed, so we set a time to meet.

At the meeting, I told the father that our team agreed his daughter was gifted in her work with children. I looked at the daughter and said, "You are a very gifted minister, specifically with special needs children." I then said to the father, "We would love to have your daughter working in the ministry once again, but there is a problem we need to address before she can return." I told the young lady that the leaders in her department had found her difficult to oversee. By insisting on doing things her own way, she created significant tension in the ministry, particularly because of her attitude toward her overseers and coworkers.

I told the father that if his daughter was going to come back, then these things would have to change. Otherwise, we could not allow her to continue working in the ministry. At first, he strongly objected to my words and came to his daughter's defense. I listened to his objections and even sympathized with some of his concerns. Then in a soft, nonconfrontational voice, I responded with some questions.

"How long have you been at Gateway Church?"
"About two years," he replied.
"Were you at another church before coming to Gateway?"
He said, "Yes, about two years."
"And before that church, were you at another church?"
He paused this time and then said, "Yes."
"How long were you at that church?

160

"About two years."

So I said to the father, "Do you see the pattern? See, I believe this problem has existed for a long time, and we were about to repeat the same things that have happened to your daughter at other churches. I'm sorry she has been treated this way by us and others, but we can stop the pattern and make this right."

I added, "I imagine that what we have experienced in our oversight and work dynamics with her has happened at each of those other churches. They too gave you the stiff arm against continued involvement in ministry, and you left."

He said, "Yes, you're right."

I then said to his daughter, "If you will let us, we will help you. We would love for your gifts to be used effectively here, but you will need to change the way you relate to others. And I believe you will need some healing." She agreed, so I asked, "Would you be willing to go to a counselor who can help you discover the root of these issues?" She said she would, and we set up a counseling relationship for her. In counseling, she discovered that she had a type of personality disorder that was treatable. She received help, and the church gained a gifted person to work with our special needs children.

It takes courage to have these kinds of conversations. Our love for people is a powerful thing when it is connected to our courage to tell them the truth. If we simply love people and respond with care that covers their unhealed areas without confronting their dysfunction, then our love becomes enabling. It permits their dysfunctional behavior and loads the burdens it creates onto the people around them. Our unwillingness to confront dysfunctional behavior hurts everyone, including the person we have enabled.

So ask yourself, *Is my love courageous or enabling?* Are you able to tell the truth and confront dysfunction with love and care in your voice and commitment in your heart? This work of pastoral leadership is essential and must be developed rather than ignored. If you are willing, God will pour courage into your heart and mind. He will assist you as you confront people with love, truth, care, and commitment. Ask Him to help you, because He will, and then be courageous in your love for people.

> Faithful are the wounds of a friend;
> profuse are the kisses of an enemy.
>
> —Proverbs 27:6

Lesson 19

BE GRACIOUS IN TRANSITION AND REMEMBER GOD IS IN CHARGE!

Do not rejoice when your enemy falls,
and let not your heart be glad when he stumbles,
lest the LORD see it and be displeased,
and turn away his anger from him.

—Proverbs 24:17–18

I press on toward the goal for the prize of the upward call of God in Christ Jesus.

—Philippians 3:14

For the gifts and the calling of God are irrevocable.

—Romans 11:29

TRANSITIONS ARE DIFFICULT. I wrote about this issue previously in Lesson 15. At this point, I will add some additional perspective on the element of change. Life is filled with change. Transition involves change and moves us from one season into another, yet change also happens within the season itself. One of the quotes Jan and I have come to embrace over many years of ministry is this: "If you don't like something, then just wait—it will change."

It will change because we have a heart to please God. He does all things with excellence. If we are failing, God won't leave us in our failure. He will lead us into change. Even when we are succeeding and God is pleased with our direction and responses, He will still lead us into change. God may even use you as a catalyst to bring about the change He wants to make in someone you oversee, pastor, or who is close to you.

At first, you may ask, "What can I do?" Then as you begin to serve, you see how things are not working. Your question changes to, "How can I help you make things different?" Remember, life has seasons, and everything in life has a limited useful timeframe. Change within a season is normal. There is a time to hold on and work to improve a program, but there is also a time to have a funeral and let things go. The biggest enemy of your tomorrow is something happening today that you refuse to allow to end.

The biggest enemy of your tomorrow is something happening today that you refuse to allow to end.

Think of this process as "pruning," which is cutting toward a vision or a desired future. The reason we prune is to enable the full expression or purpose of something and to develop it in the current season. Pruning actually needs to be a regular discipline in our lives.

A growing, healthy bush produces more buds than the plant can sustain, and so do you. At least once per year, identify what you are doing that someone around you could do. Also ask yourself, *What do I need to do that no one can do in my place?* These questions will help you identify what you need to let go of so you can be more effective in your current season.

In a pruning season, a gardener must cut away some of the good limbs of a plant or tree so that the best ones can thrive.

When we prune our lives, we most likely won't just remove things that are bad or even completely dead. Rather, we will cut some things that are good or even things we enjoy. Unless we are willing to focus our efforts on the 20 percent that is best and most life-giving, we will not be able to grow to the full measure that God wants for us.

One time in business, I went to call on a very good customer near the end of the year. I gave the usual holiday greetings and wished him a prosperous New Year. As we talked, I asked my customer if it had been a good year. He quickly responded, "Yes, it has been almost too good of a year. I am concerned." This was the first time I had heard a business-person say he was concerned because business was *too* good. He told me sales were growing so fast that his company was unable to fulfill all the orders in a timely manner. As a business leader, he realized something I needed to learn. In a growing company like his, around 20 percent of the clientele represented the life-giving bulk of his company's business. The other 80 percent was profitable, but it just wasn't the life of his company. In fact, it represented a risk that could hurt their whole business. He recognized that 80 percent of his customers threatened to dominate the executive leadership's attention, their working capital, and the personnel necessary to grow the business. The demands of the 80 percent could soon suck the resources out of the most profitable areas of the business.

The principle is this: take away the things that are distract-ing and have run their useful course, along with the things that demand resources but are not your primary focus, so that the rest may be healthy and grow. Whatever is resisting growth or not participating in it must go. These barriers to growth may be time-killers, resource-wasters, and even non-producing personnel. We must deal with the wild growing problems proac-tively to sustain healthy growth. Admit that you have done all you can to make the situation a success, but now it is time to stop and prune.

Recognize when the path you're on won't get you the result you want. A change of course is needed. You have probably heard the saying that insanity is continuing to do the same thing but expecting different results. If something isn't working, then prune it. Have the courage to cut it, remove it, and separate it. Dead branches take up space and need to be cleared away for growth. What once had life but no longer contributes needs to go. We can't hold on to non-contributing elements out of nostalgia or even a sense of loyalty. Neither can they stay for our benefit just because they give us feelings of security.

Take care not to slip into a hoarding mentality by thinking, "I might need that later." You may be convinced that as soon as you let go of something, you will need it. Consequently, you don't get rid of things when their season has come and gone. Unhealthy emotional attachment to the past will keep you from entering into the future God has for you. Do you remember Lot's wife? She had an opportunity to start a brand new life with her family, away from the evils of Sodom. However, as they were leaving, she looked back and turned into a pillar of salt (see Genesis 20).

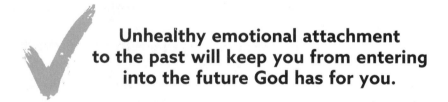

Unhealthy emotional attachment to the past will keep you from entering into the future God has for you.

God wants to trim the dead things away from your life. You may resist His trimming because it leaves you feeling exposed and vulnerable. It may even feel like the growth and beauty in an area of your life is being "clear cut," so you take a defensive posture, telling yourself that you will experience erosion and the soil of your life will be blown away. You may also be afraid that no new growth will happen for a long time. Don't let that way of thinking stand in your way. Trust God. What He clears away from your life will make the way for new growth.

In the summer of 2015, the leadership of Gateway Church began the budget process for 2016. It would be an election year, and there was a lot of uncertainty around what the future would hold for churches and other religious non-profits. The elders began to ask God what He would have us do. We collectively heard His response that we needed to prune and simplify the ministry. At first, we thought that meant we were to review the various areas of the ministry and tighten up our policies and procedures, so we embarked on that process.

Gateway Church had experienced rapid growth over its 16 years of existence. We had ballooned from approximately 300 staff members to over 900 full-time employees in just five years. We had added multiple campuses and new ministries to serve the people of the area, and we were truly helping a lot of people. We began to ask ourselves, *Are we doing the work of this ministry in the most efficient and effective way possible?*

As we began to develop the budget for 2016, we heard God say we needed to evaluate our financial stewardship as well. We observed that our finances were going well, just like the other areas of ministry. Nevertheless, they too had experienced rapid growth, and we found ourselves responsible for a great sum of revenue and assets that needed to be stewarded well. We knew we had a relatively small amount of debt compared to our assets, but we believed God was saying we needed to give attention to our debt in a very serious way.

After a careful financial review, we began to consider our personnel costs. As we did, we arrived at the conclusion that we had become overstaffed. Our discussion as elders began to focus on how to trim our staff numbers, not because we were in financial trouble but because we knew God wanted us to be good stewards in this new pruning season. The first move we made was to develop an offer to those staff members who recognized that they had come into a pruning season in their own lives and that God was leading them to make a personal change.

We began to understand that Gateway Church was coming to the end of a ministry season, and God was leading us into another. We knew we needed to stop and recognize the work that was done in the season we were in and then prepare for a new season with the right people in the right places. We asked our staff members to seek God and give an honest assessment of whether they felt their season of employment at Gateway Church was coming to an end. If God was speaking to them, then we wanted them to step forward and receive a generous transition package. We offered one month of income for every year a staff member was in service to the church, up to six months but with a minimum of two months for any person who stepped forward. Additionally, we gave special consideration to those who had served 10 years or more. That initial call for staff members to discern God's voice resulted in approximately 70 people transitioning into a new season. Some elected to retire, but most went into new places of service.

For the next step in the pruning process, we met with those who wanted to stay. Individual interviews commenced with the remaining 830 members of our staff. Each interview included a member of our executive team, a representative from our human resources department, and the individual staff member. Every person interviewed was asked these five simple questions:

1. How do you feel we are doing in this season of prune and simplify?

2. Is there anything we are doing that you think we should not be doing?
3. Is there anything we are not doing that you think we should be doing?
4. Do you feel you are in your sweet spot (your ideal place of service)?
5. Is there anything you would like to say to us as an organization?

After each interview, the human resources representative and the executive leader consulted with individual managers. We asked if we would make the choice to hire this person based on the role they currently filled in the organization. We then decided to transition individuals who did not fit what the organization would need in the new season we were entering. We didn't consider anyone to have failed. In fact, we would not have experienced the great growth we had without them. Rather, we felt this evaluation was a tangible way to discern a time for change for them as well as for us. Through this process we transitioned another 260 individuals. We offered them the same generous transition package as the first group who volunteered. Our rationale was that we wanted to thank them and help them transition to a new place of ministry and service, even as we prepared to transition to a new season as an organization.

In all transparency, almost every person saw their transition from the perspective of failure at first. One man I love and greatly respect asked me, "Please tell me what I did wrong!" I replied, "You did nothing wrong—nothing that would justify being let go." He responded, "I appreciate what you are saying, but companies do not let great people go." I then told him, "Every one of us has things that we can be coached in, but this is not about coaching; it is about a changing season."

In a changing season, we have to let go of the things from the previous season so we can grab ahold of what God has for us in the new season. Dr. Henry Cloud, author of *Necessary Endings,* consulted with us and helped us understand the truth of this perspective. The reality is that everyone had to walk a road of faith. Those who were told they were being transitioned had to trust that God was their provider and would lead them to new opportunities. This transition was not a punishment from Him or from the church leaders. For those of us who remained on staff, we had to trust that God had spoken and what these gifted people had been doing would be done through others. We also had to recalibrate some policies and procedures through our "prune and simplify" efforts. The thing about faith is that it requires us to trust God rather than what we know, see, or feel. Yes, there was a time of grief for everyone involved in the process. We all had to walk through the darkness of the unknown by faith and into the light of a new season.

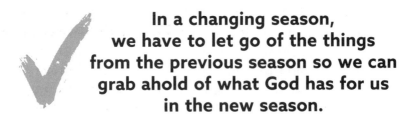

In a changing season, we have to let go of the things from the previous season so we can grab ahold of what God has for us in the new season.

Why do I relate this experience? I want to remind you that seasons of change and transition will come. I urge you to remember these simple truths as you lead people through transition:

1. God does not use transitions in our lives to punish us. His purposes are always redemptive. Even if a failure on our part

initiates a transition, God does not and will not abandon us. Encourage your people to trust God because He loves them and has good things ahead.

2. Tell them to look through the eyes of faith to see the opportunity that is before them. It will not help to look to the past or hold on to what is no more. God has good plans for them, even if they can't see those plans in the present.

3. To the extent that it is in your power, be as generous and gracious as you possibly can with those under your care who are being transitioned. Love them, care for them, and if they will let you, walk with them into their new season. When they look back, they will thank God for the transition and for His sustaining love that came to them through you.

4. Change is good and necessary. Instead of resisting it, choose to make the best of it. Encourage them to trust God, be gracious to others, and don't blame a boss or leader for the transition.

Are you in transition right now? Are you leading someone into a transition? Don't panic or resist the change that is coming. Ride the wave of the change and embrace it. Help others to do the same. Change is a normal part of life, and God will use it in powerful ways.

Bear one another's burdens, and so fulfill the law of Christ. For if anyone thinks he is something, when he is nothing, he deceives himself. But let each one test his own work, and then his reason to boast will be in himself alone and not in his neighbor. For each will have to bear his own load.

—Galatians 6:2–5

Lesson 20

WATCH YOUR SIX—AT ALL TIMES!

Be sober-minded; be watchful. Your adversary the devil prowls around like a roaring lion, seeking someone to devour. Resist him, firm in your faith, knowing that the same kinds of suffering are being experienced by your brotherhood throughout the world.

—1 Peter 5:8–9

For we do not wrestle against flesh and blood, but against the rulers, against the authorities, against the cosmic powers over this present darkness, against the spiritual forces of evil in the heavenly places. Therefore take up the whole armor of God, that you may be able to withstand in the evil day, and having done all, to stand firm.

—Ephesians 6:12–13

ANYONE WHO HAS been in the military is familiar with the warning, "Watch your six!" This statement of warning is based on the image of the numbers on a clock; if you were facing twelve, then six would be at your back. It is a way to communicate to fellow soldiers to look out behind them. If you're in a battle for your life, then there's no time to deliver a twenty-five-word warning. The caution needs to be short and quick because lives depend on it.

Most of us have encountered this warning outside the military as well. It is now embedded in the common vernacular and reminds us that some significant things may be going on in our blind spots. *We all have blind spots.*

We should all remember that some activity may be happening behind us that we have forgotten about or can't see because it is out of our line of sight. "Watch your six" can also serve as a cryptic warning that someone may be actively plotting against you or working behind your back to cause you harm. It is a reminder not to turn your back on your enemies, because they are always looking for weaknesses or vulnerable places in your character. They want to find gaps in your defenses to do you harm as they launch unexpected attacks. In all these cases, "watch your six" conveys a warning to stay alert, be on guard, and don't forget that you are in a spiritual war.

In his book *Embedded Enemy: The Insider Threat,* Bart Womack relates the true story of Sergeant Hasan Akbar, an American soldier in Iraq. This is an account of the deadly attack against the men and women of Headquarters and Headquarters Company First Brigade, 101st Airborne Division. The Bastogne Brigade was staged at Camp Pennsylvania in Kuwait, where they prepared for combat. During the early morning hours of March 23, 2003, Sergeant Akbar did the unthinkable—he single-handedly led an inside attack on U.S. forces by throwing hand grenades into his chain of command's tents while they slept. In the panic that ensued, Akbar then followed up his attack with small-arms fire as his commanding officers tried to flee their sleeping quarters. That day they didn't go into combat—it came to them, unexpectedly.

As Christ followers, we must always be aware that we are in a war. Our combat is spiritual, and it has eternal life and death consequences. The apostle Paul wrote that we do not battle against flesh and blood, even though an attack may come in a physical form. It has an unseen spiritual commander who deploys principalities, spiritual powers, and rulers from the unseen realm with a systematic strategy bent on our destruction

(Ephesians 6:12). This unseen enemy will often work through people and circumstances to wage war against us.

Our combat is spiritual, and it has eternal life and death consequences.

In the larger picture, our enemy is really attempting to wage war against our heavenly Father, although he is no match. Satan's insurgency started before Creation. The prophet Isaiah records these events. He tells about the time when Lucifer became puffed up with pride and sought to overthrow God Himself. Lucifer's aspiration was to be like Him through establishing his own rule and domain (Isaiah 14:13–14). So God cast him down from heaven, and thus began the battle that continues today. You and I are God's beloved creation, so Satan tries to bring us into the battle too. Ultimately, he wants us to follow him rather than God. Satan absolutely hates it when we submit our lives to the Lord, and because he sees us as his enemy, he is hellbent on our destruction.

The apostle Peter wrote, "Be sober-minded; be watchful. Your adversary the devil prowls around like a roaring lion, seeking someone to devour" (1 Peter 5:8). God wants us to be on guard because the enemy will use every secret and covert way he can to wreak havoc on us. The devil wants to ruin our reputations and our influence, destroy our marriages, and lead our children away from the Lord. He would love to saddle our children with addictions and mark them for destruction. If the enemy can get us to relax our guard, then he thinks he can ultimately destroy us.

Yes, our enemy is shrewd, crafty, and patient, but he knows he has no real authority. Jesus was able to disarm him with

God's Word and defeat him on the cross (Colossians 2:15). The devil's power to destroy comes from his attempts to deceive us into destroying ourselves. How does he do this? He tries to get us to move out from under God's protective canopy of grace. Satan will appeal to our "free will" to live, act, and react on our own, apart from God's direct care and guidance. The devil will try to lull us into a false sense of safety, and then he will unleash the full force of his destructive power. He wants to bring the battle straight to us by working through our inner thoughts and outward actions. He gets us to imagine and act in ways we never would have thought possible.

I first learned about Satan's tricks while I was living in Amarillo and working for my father's business. I was a novice in spiritual warfare at the time. I took a position as the sales representative for our company and tried to get our customers to purchase our products. I knew that I loved God. I was happily married with two children, and we were buying a house (living the American dream). I was surrounded by good friends, and I actively attended and worked in a local church. If you were to ask me, I would have told you that I lived within a "safe zone," insulated from the enemy's attacks. Out of my safe environment, I went into the world to fight the fight. I really didn't expect the enemy to bring the fight to me.

It happened to be summer, and with the warmer temperatures, women were wearing more revealing clothing. Now, I love my wife and am committed to her for life. I am also thankful for our family and would never consider being unfaithful to her. However, I started to take on a lazy attitude regarding my thought life and how I looked at other women. I thought, *What does it hurt to look?* I was safe behind my love and commitment to my wife and my good life, right?

I stopped to make a sales presentation of a new product with a hotel customer and hopefully take an order. As I walked through the lobby toward the reception desk to ask for the manager, an airline flight crew was checking into the hotel at the same time. The pilots and three female flight attendants gathered around the check-in desk. I greeted them and made an offhanded remark about the heat. Then I said it would be a good day to lay by the pool. It was an innocent comment, and I was just being friendly—or so I thought.

The manager soon emerged and greeted me. We stepped away from the desk into the middle of the lobby to continue our conversation. As we stood there talking, the flight crew passed by on their way to the grand stairway and toward their rooms. As they were ascending the stairs, one of the flight attendants paused and turned toward me. As I peered over the manager's shoulder, she made eye contact and motioned for me to follow her to her room. I was admittedly stunned by the gesture. I probably looked like Deputy Barney Fife from Mayberry when he tried to confront a bank robber. I stumbled over my words as I tried to finish my conversation with the manager. I couldn't wait to retreat to the safety of my car.

It was that day I began to understand that I was in a spiritual battle. I gained a new perspective on the enemy's covert efforts. He wanted to catch me sleeping with my guard down. That day I knew what James was writing about in his epistle: "Blessed is the man who remains steadfast under trial, for when he has stood the test he will receive the crown of life, which God has promised to those who love him" (James 1:12). I realized then that the enemy plays a long game as he seeks our ultimate destruction. He knows we will immediately recognize a front-on, undisguised attack and will meet it with resistance. So he slowly and subtly introduces bits of tempting stimuli to encourage us to feel secure in our commitments to the Lord and others. We feel safe, even while he is appealing to our appetites. You see, our enemy is fully aware of the way God created us. God gave us appetites for food, knowledge, status, sex, pleasure, and purpose. These appetites are not wrong in themselves; each one plays an important part in helping us live the lives God intends for us. In His Word, God has given us the outline for how we are to satisfy those appetites. His method provides health and life. He wants us to be physically, emotionally, and spiritually healthy, and He always wants what is best for us.

On the other hand, the enemy makes a play for our appetites when we are most vulnerable. He waits and watches for us to become hungry or tired, and then he tries to convince us that the most important thing we can do in the moment is satisfy our hunger and relieve our fatigue by any means available. No matter what the appetite is, his appeal is the same: "You don't need to wait. If you do, then you might die. What you need is refreshing comfort. Here, try this. It will satisfy and renew you." The enemy's attempts to get us to satisfy our God-given appetites always come in a way of which God doesn't approve. The devil wants us to lust—to have a strong desire to satisfy our appetites through immediate action. His solutions are always nearsighted with disastrous consequences. The strength of his appeal begins to weigh on our thoughts, raise our heart rates, and attempts to get us to act with urgency. Once a decision is conceived in our minds and hearts, then we act without consideration of God's plan for us or the consequences the action will produce. We sin. Sin leads to separation from God, and without repentance, it will lead to our spiritual death. No one is safe from the enemy's game; no one is immune.

FIGHT AND FIGHT WELL

So how are we to respond to the enemy's attacks? *We are to fight and fight well.* Either we do, or we will be hurt in the battle and possibly destroyed. We must put on the armor of God, which the apostle Paul lists in Ephesians 6. We must walk with other believers who will help us be transparent and accountable.

We must walk with other believers who will help us be transparent and accountable.

Pastor Jack Hayford said that one day he walked into his office reception area and greeted one of the ladies with a hug. As he continued into his office, he thought to himself, *That felt really good! I think I would like another.* Then Pastor Jack said, "So, I walked across the hall into the office of my associate and told him what had just happened and how I felt." Through that action, Pastor Jack exposed the enemy's appeal to his appetite and defeated the strategy aimed at his destruction.

REMAIN SOBER-MINDED

We are to remain sober-minded. By that I mean we should be diligently aware of the surrounding dangers involved with all our activities. I will consider the consequences of my actions and their impact on my reputation and influence. I will be especially mindful of their effect on my intimacy with God. I will have a disciplined awareness of my vulnerability and motives, and I will make careful choices about the people with whom I associate and the activities in which I participate.

I have had the privilege of knowing a few professional athletes over the years. Each of them had a common life commitment, regardless of the sport. As they lived away from their sport, whether during the season or the off-season, they would carefully consider their extracurricular involvements. They would not allow themselves to be teased or taunted into doing something that might result in injury or risk their teams' reputations (and thereby jeopardize their careers). That meant they refused to engage in some "fun" activities. Their commitment to their professions, teams, and careers required them to keep watch and guard what was important to them. We too must live with that kind of discipline so we will not risk the reputation or influence God has given to us. We must always be ready to fight against the enemy and defeat his every attack.

SURROUND YOURSELF WITH ALLIES

Yes, watch your six. When you live engaged in God's purposes, you need committed and close relationships with a team who will surround you. These should be people who care about you and know you well enough to call out the good in you and warn you of the bad. They will caution you when danger is present, giving you a heads up and telling you, "Watch your six!" Your team should begin with your spouse and extend to a few committed friends. In a formal way it should include account-ability to someone God has put in authority over you, such as your pastor, boss, or possibly a board of directors. "Watching your six" begins by declaring and submitting your activities to those who stand watch with you and over you so they won't have to come to your rescue when you get in trouble by acting independently and wandering into Satan's trap.

As you head out to face this day, watch your six. The enemy has you in his sights!

Blessed is the man who remains steadfast under trial, for when he has stood the test he will receive the crown of life, which God has promised to those who love him.

—James 1:12

Lesson 21

FINISH STRONG AND DON'T COAST TO THE FINISH LINE!

This Book of the Law shall not depart from your mouth, but you shall meditate on it day and night, so that you may be careful to do according to all that is written in it. For then you will make your way prosperous, and then you will have good success. Have I not commanded you? Be strong and courageous. Do not be frightened, and do not be dismayed, for the LORD your God is with you wherever you go."

—Joshua 1:8–9

Only let your manner of life be worthy of the gospel of Christ, so that whether I come and see you or am absent, *I may hear of you that you are standing firm in one spirit,* with one mind striving side by side for the faith of the gospel, and not frightened in anything by your opponents. This is a clear sign to them of their destruction, but of your salvation, and that from God. For it has been granted to you that for the sake of Christ you should not only believe in him but also suffer for his sake, engaged in the same conflict that you saw I had and now hear that I still have.

—Philippians 1:27–30, emphasis added

By this all people will know that you are my disciples, if you have love for one another.

—John 13:35

And have you forgotten the exhortation that addresses you as sons?
"My son, do not regard lightly the discipline of the Lord,
    nor be weary when reproved by him.
For the Lord disciplines the one he loves,
    and chastises every son whom he receives."

—Hebrews 12:5–6

Likewise, you who are younger, be subject to the elders. Clothe yourselves, all of you, with humility toward one another, for "God opposes the proud but gives grace to the humble." Humble yourselves, therefore, under the mighty hand of God so that at the proper time he may exalt you, casting all your anxieties on him, because he cares for you.

—1 Peter 5:5–7

WHAT DOES IT mean to "finish strong"? Many sports analogies come to mind as I consider this phrase. However, it means to give every effort all the way to the end. Finishing strong doesn't necessarily mean we will have accumulated more or performed better than everyone else when we reach the end of our race. In fact, we recognize that we can't finish the race on our own at all. We need help along the way. Only one person has ever finished perfectly, and that is Jesus Himself (see Hebrews 12:1–2). We must put our faith and trust in His work on our behalf and give our best effort so we will hear Him say, "Well done, good and faithful servant."

We have examples to draw from as we are running life's race. We have the stories of people from the Bible, people throughout history, and people around us. We can learn from Abraham Lincoln, who was motivated to finish strong by a friend. Lincoln said, "I'm a success today because I had a friend who believed in me and I didn't have the heart to let him down." We can follow Winston Churchill, who encouraged others to "never give in except to convictions of honour and good sense." And we can read the words of Helen Keller, who was encouraged to finish strong by this thought: "Character cannot be developed in ease and quiet. Only through the experience of trial and suffering can the soul be strengthened, ambition inspired, and success achieved."

We recognize that we can't finish the race on our own at all. We need help along the way.

The writer of Hebrews instructs,

> Let us run with endurance the race that is set before us, looking to Jesus, the founder and perfecter of our faith, who for the joy that was set before him endured the cross, despising the shame, and is seated at the right hand of the throne of God (Hebrews 12:1–2).

As Christ followers, we know it is impossible to please God without faith (see Hebrews 11:6). Real faith is never static; instead, it leads us to act because God is speaking to and working in us. We are convinced that He rewards those who seek, love, and serve Him.

The Bible records the accounts of some great heroes of the faith who performed mighty exploits under God's power because they heard, believed, and obeyed His commands and directions. As they followed Him, He blessed and used them in mighty and powerful ways, acting miraculously on their behalf. However, many of these same people lost their focus and did not finish strong. Men such as Gideon, David, Samson, and Solomon were great in their exploits, but they did not finish strong in their devotion and service to God. Why did this happen? I believe the reason is an improper pace that leads to burnout.

I began playing sports when I was eight years old, and I participated in organized sports all the way through high school. I was best at playing football. Growing up in Nebraska, I dreamed of playing football for the Cornhuskers of the University of Nebraska. Although I was an honorable mention all-state defensive end, my coaches told me I was not big enough to play Division I college football. Some Division II schools tried to recruit me, and I really considered playing for one of them. I even went on a recruiting trip to a school, worked out with the players, and met the coaches. While I was in the process of making my decision, one of my high school coaches offered to train me over the summer and help me get ready for my freshman year as a Division II college player. However, I was already tired and burned out from the devotion it took to succeed at the high school level. College sports, even at the Division II level, would require even more devotion and commitment. So I decided I was done living my life for sports. My heart was not in the workouts that would prepare me for fall football. I did not have it in me to carry on the effort at that level.

As a pastor, I have witnessed many Christ followers express their love for God in both service and commitment to a local body of believers. They serve faithfully for many years with burning hot commitment and devotion to Christ, but then they begin to feel discouraged, worn out, and frustrated. At some point they lose the desire to engage at a new level of spiritual competition because with each new level come new demons to confront and resist. They no longer have the heart to do what it takes to fight, resist, and compete. Like I did with football, they conclude that they are done. It is as if they decide to retire from service to God. They go inactive in their service and experience a shipwreck of faith. Paul warned Timothy about this potential condition and encouraged him to "wage the good warfare, holding faith and a good conscience" (1 Timothy 1:18).

There are others who remain firm in their love for God, but they simply withdraw from active service, stand on the sidelines, and then coast to the finish line. What a tragedy! Some believers start strong, but just as they are turning onto the final lap of the race, they lose the heart and dedication they once had. Instead of getting their second wind and pressing toward the finish line, they end up broken down on the sideline. Don't let that be your story!

As followers and servants of Christ, our goal should be to hear our Lord say, "Well done, good and faithful servant!" We willingly join the race He has prepared for us to run. Run your race—not someone else's—and remind yourself often that it's a marathon rather than a sprint. When you have a bad day or are confronted with a failed effort, pick yourself up, dust yourself off, and run again. Remember the acronym F.I.D.O. that I introduced in Lesson 7? Say that to yourself often and remind yourself to do the right thing no matter what happens. Encourage yourself in the midst of disappointment to "Forget it and Drive on!"

Run your race—not someone else's— and remind yourself often that it's a marathon rather than a sprint.

My dad told me never to view my career from the perspective of a single day. You will have good days when everything is working, and you can't seem to mess anything up or do anything

187

wrong. You hope those days never end. They make you feel like you're a genius who has received God's special favor, anointing, and blessing. If you focus on those days, then you may move in the direction of pride and arrogance. They will snuff out humility and appreciation for the opportunities given to you. They will ultimately kill the heart of servanthood in you as you become puffed up and begin attributing your success to your own abilities and contributions.

Yes, you should thank God for the good days, but know this: in every life a little rain will come. Days will come when nothing seems to be working. Discouragement will begin to set in, and the enemy will whisper, "You should just quit." He will tell you that you've lost God's anointing and favor. When those bad days come, it will feel as though they will never end. One difficult day seems to stretch into a month or longer. If you allow those days to transform your perspective about your career, then they will rob you of confidence and faith and cause you to question your purpose. Your change in attitude will produce instability in you and lead you to embrace career changes that are out of step with God's timing.

Remember to view your life and career from the perspective of a marathoner. Focus your thoughts on thankfulness, diligence, faithfulness, and a pace that produces endurance. You will want to finish your race with enough energy to "kick it" to the finish line. That is what it means to finish strong.

HOW TO FINISH THE RACE

I will leave you with three helpful ways you can finish the race well. If you will devote yourself to them, then you will be successful.

MAKE GOD YOUR FOCUS

Focus on God in all things. Remember, He is the real prize and not fame, satisfaction of your appetites, pleasure, or indulgence. You will not "win" by collecting material things or wealth. Point your desires every day to how you will pursue and fulfill God's will. Love others the way you love yourself. Practice the Golden Rule and do for them what you want done for yourself.

VALUE RELATIONSHIPS

Give relationships priority over issues. Remember that we can take only one thing into eternity, and that is the relationships we have built here on earth. Relationships are eternal; make every effort to show you value them. Determine to resolve misunderstandings, walk in forgiveness, and be kind and gracious to everyone you encounter. Value the gifts of others and their contributions to God's work. Psalm 133 tells us God pours out His blessing and provides life when there is unity. Place unity above all else and protect it as if you are guarding Fort Knox.

Unity does not equate to conformity; rather, it is produced through loving and honest communication. Openly and passionately share your perspectives on issues while also working to build unity and common understanding. You will want a shared positive outcome for the decisions you are making.

WALK IN ACCOUNTABILITY

You need one or more godly mentors to whom you will be accountable. Submit yourself willingly to them and openly disclose your thoughts and plans before you act on them. Have these conversations when things are going well and especially when things are difficult. No matter how sharp, intelligent, experienced, or knowledgeable you may be, you must remember *you don't know everything!*

Realize you have the capacity to make mistakes. You could be blind to a situation or foolishly naive in your perspective. Even worse, you may accidentally mess things up and cause unintended harm to yourself and others. Seek input before making decisions. Make it your goal to gain permission rather than forgiveness. Don't go rogue on any of your decisions; instead, walk in accountability. King Solomon wrote,

> For by wise counsel you will wage your own war,
> And in a multitude of counselors *there is* safety
> (Proverbs 24:6 NKJV).

Make it your goal to gain permission rather than forgiveness.

It is easier to correct a mistake before it happens than to repair it once the damage has been done. Accept correction and discipline with humility and appreciation. The writer of Hebrews tells us to endure discipline: "For what son is there whom his father does not discipline?" (Hebrews 12:7). The pain of discipline is intended to remind us of the lesson we are learning so we will not repeat the same mistakes. Correction may be painful for a moment, but it will guide you for a lifetime.

Where are you in your race? Are you tired? Are you sitting on the sideline in discouragement or frustration? Choose today to get up, move forward, and finish strong.

> Therefore, my beloved, as you have always obeyed, so now, not only as in my presence but much more in my absence,

work out your own salvation with fear and trembling, *for it is God who works in you, both to will and to work for his good pleasure.*

—Philippians 2:12–13, emphasis added

ABOUT THE AUTHOR

TOM LANE IS the apostolic senior pastor of Gateway Church in the Dallas/Fort Worth Metroplex. He oversees the Outreach Ministries of Gateway Church, which include The Kings University, Gateway Global Ministry, Kingdom Business Leaders, and Gateway Church Network. Tom works with the executive teams in each of these ministry areas to execute the vision and values of the church. Prior to this position, he served as Gateway Church's executive senior pastor for 12 years and as the Dallas campus pastor for two years.

Tom's vocational ministry experience spans more than 37 years. Before joining the staff at Gateway Church, he served at Trinity Fellowship Church in Amarillo, Texas. Tom has experience in a variety of church leadership roles, including business administrator, administrative pastor, executive pastor, and senior pastor.

Tom's extensive ministry expertise and engaging relational style bring a warmth to his speaking, writing, and pastoral ministry. He is the author and co-author of several books, including *Heritage, A Father's Influence to the Generations, Foundations of Healthy Church Government, He Still Speaks, Strong Women and the Men Who Love Them, Conversations with God,* and *Letters from a Dad to a Graduate.*

Tom and his wife, Jan, have been married for over 40 years. They have four married children and 15 grandchildren.

Get the companion guide:

ISBN: 978-1-951227-43-2
www.gatewaypublishing.com

MORE FROM TOM LANE

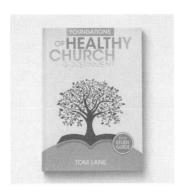

Foundations of Healthy Church Government

Develop an enduring, biblical model of governance for your church, reignite growth, and move your staff and vision from confusion to unity.

Book: 9781945529306

Heritage: A Father's Influence to the Generations

Tom Lane provides practical tools, biblical foundation, and inspiration for imparting godly character to the generations entrusted to you.

Book: 9781945529399
DVD: 9781949399455

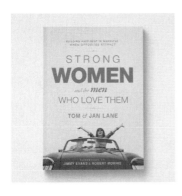

Strong Women and the Men Who Love Them

Using principles and perspectives based in Scripture, couples will learn to appreciate the expression of each person's gifts to benefit the relationship.

Book: 9781629985923
Study Guide: 9781945529771

 GATEWAY® PRESS

www.gatewaypublishing.com